FULNESS OF JOY

Other works by the author

A Hidden Fire
Deeper Into God
Christian Spirituality Series:
Praying the Jesus Prayer
The Stations of the Cross
Life's Changing Seasons
Praying the Bible

FULNESS OF JOY

The Presence of God in Human Life

by

Brother Ramon SSF

Marshall Pickering

Marshall Morgan and Scott
Marshall Pickering
3 Beggarwood Lane, Basingstoke, Hants RG23 7LP, UK

First published in 1988 by Marshall Morgan and Scott
Publications Ltd
Part of the Marshall Pickering Holdings Group
A subsidiary of the Zondervan Corporation

ISBN 0-551-01602-7

Text Set in Plantin by Brian Robinson, Buckingham
Printed in Great Britain by Richard Clay Ltd, Bungay, Suffolk

For the joy of hospitality and quiet in the
writing of this book,
with Ieuan and Margaret Lloyd, at St George's Square,
Worcester,
the Community of St Clare, Freeland, Oxford,
and the patient friars at Glasshampton Monastery,
Worcester,
thanks and praise!

and for my dear parents
David and Edna
both of whom died as this book was going to press.

'In Thy presence there is Fulness of Joy'.

Contents

Introduction: The Direction of the Pilgrimage

Joy is immediate, first-hand, intensely personal and powerfully corporate. It is dynamic and tranquil, explosive and gentle, manifesting itself in blazing glory or profound contemplation. Already I am caught up in paradoxes when speaking of the essence of joy.

It would not have come to me to write directly on the theme of joy; I would have approached it obliquely in dealing with the great experiences of human life. But having been asked to write, I find myself 'enjoying' the experience of living with the theme in prayer, thought and study.

From the outset, it is clear that I cannot divorce joy from sorrow. It can only be experienced and communicated in its profound depth and high ecstasy when painted upon the larger canvas of the totality of human existence. The light and glory of joy is seen in all its beauty only when the darker shades and tones of sorrow and suffering are contained within the canvas, for the whole of human life is the background of joy. Honesty and integrity demand the whole picture, and the wonderful thing is that joy is more accessible, and its potential more possible, when the story of pain and sorrow are told alongside it.

St Irenaeus, martyred at Lyons around AD 200, wrote: 'The glory of God is man fully alive, for man's true life is the vision of God.' This is the beautiful quotation which is before me as I write, because Irenaeus exemplified the Gospel in his fully human life and death for Christ, and thus encountered joy. And that joy encompasses the whole of human life, the totality of human experience, with all its problems and pain, with all its loveliness and ecstasies. Even martyrdom could be counted all joy! To be fully alive is the experience of joy, and such an experience culminates in the vision of God, both here and hereafter.

This book is written from a life of prayer, study and teaching in a contemplative monastery, and from a varied ecumenical ministry in churches, and hitch-hiking on the motorway network around the country. Therefore it is less an academic investigation than a pilgrimage of enquiry and devotion. I feel it is a great privilege to be an heir of the profound monastic tradition while sharing and communicating the Gospel to all manner of people both 'sacred and secular'. I commend, in this book, a contemplative attitude to the world, and each chapter leads to a meditation and a simple course of action, so that the contemplation overflows in dynamic love. To say that one loves God without compassion for the world is empty hypocrisy.

The first section deals with the *wellsprings of joy*. This earths the experience of joy within creation itself, giving priority to the life, light and love which are at the heart of the created order. The cosmos is alive and dancing, and that movement, rhythm, pattern and design are the gifts of God's continual creation as he communicates himself in the material world.

Having affirmed the world as good, and creation as originally innocent and life-giving, it becomes necessary to face up to the grim realities of evil and suffering – of alienation in some of its forms. The old divines used to speak of 'original sin', but the Genesis narrative reveals love and innocence as original. Sin is therefore invasive, parasitical, and alienation is something imposed upon an original goodness. Such alienation is the loss of joy, and right from the beginning, the recovery of joy in redemption is envisaged. Jesus is 'the lamb slain before the foundation of the world' – he saves us before we fall! This is sound Franciscan theology – the compassion of God was at work from the very beginning. The first section therefore concludes with a consideration of the source of all joy – which is the triune love of God. Loss and restoration by the grace of the divine Love is beautifully expressed in the penitential psalm *Miserere*:

> Create in me a clean heart, O God,
> and put a new and right spirit within me.
> Cast me not away from thy presence,
> and take not thy Holy Spirit from me.
> Restore to me the joy of thy salvation,
> and uphold me with a willing spirit.

The second section of the book deals with *the context of joy*. This is where I want to explore a little of what St Irenaeus means when he speaks of the glory of God being manifested in a man fully alive.* The questions which arise here are concerned with what it means to be truly human. What is the joy that we should be experiencing here and now? What are we capable of potentially, and what are our untapped sources of vital life? What does it mean to be aware of both the personal and corporate dimensions of human life, and how can the exciting adventure of the contemplative life open up for every human person? These are questions which many secular people feel can no longer be asked, let alone answered.

The final section is an invitation to *the experience of joy*. When we affirm the inheritance of our humanity, in the depths of its pain and the height of its joy, we become aware of spiritual vitality in our experience. This section is an exploration of the dying and rising principle which is found at the heart of creation, as well as in the passion and glory of our Lord Jesus Christ. This means really and honestly facing up to what we were intended to be, what alienating experiences have happened to us along the way, and how we can regain those life-giving energies which are our inheritance in nature and in grace. It goes on to share the ways in which such joy can be communicated to others in the sense in which St

Seraphim said that if the believer is indwelt by the Holy Spirit he will be filled with joy, and those around him will become aware of God's living presence.

The vitality of such joy will then be traced in the experience of life and death, coming to see what St Francis meant by embracing physical death as his sister, and seeing it in the whole context of creation and re-creation. This will bring us to the borderland of physical death and the larger life in Christ in which we shall say what we can about eternal joy, which is the new beginning of a fuller existence in which the personal and the corporate are caught up into the eternal dance of God throughout unending ages of joy and glory which is the consummation of all things.

This is truly a large canvas, and though I am unable to deal adquately with it, I have glimpsed enough of it to set me alight with joy and with pain, and if I can share some of my glimpses, it will establish both the writer and the reader in the fulness of joy which is here and to come.

Brother Ramon SSF
The Society of St Francis
Easter, 1988

**Man* is a generic term here, and throughout the book where the sense calls for it. Men *and* women constitute the wholeness of our humanity.

PART I:

The Wellsprings of Joy

1 Creation: The Dance of Joy

The Universal Presence

Some years ago, while doing theological work at Edinburgh University and living with the Community of the Transfiguration, I cycled one afternoon down past Roslin Castle and into the Glen. It was a beautiful day towards the end of summer. I propped my bike against a tree, wandered down the valley, absorbing the solitude, and listened to the gurgling waters of the burn below. Eventually I found a shady spot and sat against a tree, opening my mind and heart in an intuitive and receptive realisation of God's living presence at the heart of the created order.

I became aware of my identity with the tree which towered above me, sending its roots into the earth below. I thought of the roots deriving sustenance and moisture from the good earth, and felt the rising of the sap up into the trunk, along its branches and spreading throughout its foliage. I raised and lifted myself through the tree to receive the sunshine and rain, to live in the clean and clear air of Roslin Glen, and felt the life-giving sap of the Holy Spirit rising within me. This contemplative attitude gave way to prayer and praise, and then to silence and adoration, a resting in the God who was present at the heart of his creation.

This is an illustration of an intuitive participation in the dance of joy which is the creative presence of God in his world. The first four verses of the Bible speak of God the Father creating, speaking his eternal Word, and moving and breathing by his life-giving Spirit into the primaeval darkness and chaos. The earth, which was 'without form and void', became alive with the life, harmony, order and design of

God, manifesting his glory and reciprocating praise and adoration.

This is not pantheism, but a contemplative understanding of the doctrine of the immanence of God taught by patriarch, prophet, seer, psalmist and apostle, and less appreciated in the Western Church than in the Eastern. If pantheism teaches that God is the sum of all created things, and that the created order exhausts the being of God, then that is not what I am affirming here. God is the ever-present One. He does not change, does not 'come' and 'go' from one place to another, for as the psalmist cries:

> Whither shall I go from thy Spirit? Or whither shall I flee from thy presence? If I ascend to heaven, thou art there! If I make my bed in Sheol, thou art there! If I take the wings of the morning and dwell in the uttermost parts of the sea, even there thy hand shall lead me, and thy right hand shall hold me.[1]

This is not only an expression of a contemplative attitude towards the created order, but also a comforting doctrine in days of darkness and pain. In some of Dylan Thomas's portrayals of Puritan nonconformity a typical Welsh bedroom would have a framed text above the doublebed, reading 'Thou, God, seest me', in order to provoke fear and godly respectability among the religious community. But the old doctrines of the omniscience and omnipresence of God, at least as portrayed in Psalm 139, are doctrines which are born out of the living experience of divine holiness and love. Because the psalmist writes out of direct and living experience of God, he cries out in adoration and praise. Joy mingles with wonder as he allows his soul to be exposed to the blazing scrutiny of the divine mystery and love:

> Search me, O God, and know my heart! Try me and know my thoughts! And see if there be any wicked way in me, and lead me in the way everlasting.[2]

Abhishiktananda, the Belgian Benedictine monk, out of his many years of Christian life in India, writes concerning what he calls the Holy Presence:

> God is always present to us. There is no time and no place in our daily life or occupations in which God is not present to us; there are not even certain times or occupations in which God is more present to us or less present to us. God is always the same, the Almighty, the Infinite, the Eternal . . . Everywhere and always He is, He is Himself in His fulness; there is no sense in which He can be more 'here' or less 'there' since He is indivisible. In truth, it is to Himself alone that God is ever present. From eternity He is for Himself and in Himself. He enjoys for ever the unspeakable bliss of His Presence to Himself, the Presence of the Father to the Son and of the Son to the Father, and the mutual Presence of both to the Holy Spirit. This mystery is revealed to us by Jesus Himself, out of His experience as Son of God (John 14:10,11,16; 15:10,26; 16:13,14; 17:5, 22–24).
>
> Creation is simply the communication of this Presence, this mysterious life of God in Himself. Everything that exists, every being that lives and thinks, does so by sharing in His Being, His divine life and self-awareness. It is from and through this very Presence of God to Himself that all creatures exist, that living creatures are born and grow, that man is aware of himself, and finally becomes an individual being, endowed with a personal call and vocation for time and eternity.[3]

In this first chapter I want to affirm the joy of God's presence at the heart of his creation, and the possibility of experiencing that joy. There is no place where God is not – he is the centre whose circumference is nowhere. Because of this, the believer is able to experience the joy of God in creation mirrored in the depths of his own being. He is then able to recognise and affirm the biblical revelation of that creative joy reflected in the whole panorama of the biblical tradition, and in the Church's evangelical and mystical tradition. And then he is able to share personally and corporately that joy in all creative and redemptive experiences in which God's love is manifested.

Of course, there is a problem that immediately confronts us – it is the problem of suffering, of evil. Why is it that the divine presence is not universally recognised, celebrated and adored? Why is it that to deny the being of God, especially the God of creative love, is so easy in a world like this? Indeed, if God is universally present, and his love is at the heart of his creation, then why is the world like this?

These questions will be taken up in the next chapter, because the primary task is to affirm that joy and love are basic, are of the essence of creation. It is a sad commentary on our world that many people have no other place from which to begin than their own alienation, their own sadness, sickness or despair. This is the condition in which they find themselves. And this is the very place where the Gospel of Christ is able to reach them with its message of forgiveness, love and power. But before we plunge into the darkness of sin and alienation, the basic and primary truth of God's creative love needs to be affirmed. God's love and joy expressed in creation are primary, sin and suffering are invasive and parasitical. We shall come back to this, for it is vitally important for a correct understanding of God's redeeming and rescuing love which restores to us the paradise which we have lost. But first we must continue the affirmation of God's immanence in the created order, and the possibility of our experience of it.

My own experience of the immanence of God was not the result of a cerebral or intellectual acceptance of a piece of Christian dogma. I felt and intuited the mystery of God's being and love as a child. The divine mystery flowed into my childhood experience and I reciprocated in embracing that felt mystery. I did not differentiate between physical, mental and spiritual experience as a child – the unity of my being and experience was an immediate awareness. Only much later did I differentiate and categorise.

The presence of God and its manifestation

There is a difference between *affirming* the presence of God and *experiencing* the manifestion of that presence. Moses was certainly within the divine presence in the wilderness, though he was unaware of it until God manifested that presence from the glory of the bush which burned without being consumed.[4] Elizabeth Barrett Browning states it succinctly:

> Earth's crammed with heaven,
> And every common bush afire with God;
> But only he who sees takes off his shoes,
> The rest sit round it and pluck blackberries.[5]

Jacob was wandering in the wilderness, fleeing from his brother Esau, and seeking a pattern in his pilgrimage. He was not aware of the guiding providence of God, nor was he aware that God's living presence was everywhere about him. Weary, he took a stone for a pillow in a deserted place and went to sleep. Then came the dream – and how important dreams are both in holy scripture and in contemporary applied psychiatric practice. Jacob saw a ladder of commerce between earth and heaven, with angelic beings ascending and descending, and the voice and revelation of God spoke to him from the midst of the mystery. Jacob's reaction when waking indicates the difference between the *presence* and the *manifestation* of the presence of God, when he said: 'Surely the Lord is in this place; and I did not know it.' And he was afraid, and said, 'How awesome is this place! This is none other than the house of God, and this is the gate of heaven.'[6]

God is actually *here* – and we do not know it – we are not aware of it! There is an even sadder thing: some men do know, and try to run away. Do you remember?:

> Now the word of the Lord came to Jonah the Son of Amittai, saying, 'Arise, go to Nineveh, that great city, and cry against it; for their wickedness has come up before me.' But Jonah rose to flee to Tarshish from the presence of the Lord . . .[7]

But he wasn't successful! In his case the Hound of Heaven was on his track, but that is the theme we shall return to later.

There are, of course, occasions when the Lord hides himself away in inscrutable mystery, sometimes stimulating the lover to seek him all the more earnestly and intensely, but just now we are concerned with the open secret that God is, and that he manifests himself to the seeking and believing heart. There is a revelation of his being, his character, his holiness and his love, and it is at the heart of creation, and confirmed in redemption.

This is no strange or foreign god – no faraway deity who has wound up the mechanism of his creation, allowing it to tick on, with irregular interferences to make repairs. This is the God who is wholly ours, who dwells most intimately at the heart of the cosmos and desires to dwell even more intimately within the human heart. Abhishiktananda makes the point that man is unique among the creatures of earth because he is called into fellowship and union with God – to reciprocate such awareness in contemplative prayer:

> Man, alone among creatures, has the privilege of being aware of this Presence and of being called to reciprocate it; that is, he is called to be present to God as God is present to him, in the way in which, within the Blessed Trinity, the Son of God is eternally present to the Father as the Father is present to Him. Did not Jesus assure us that our relationship with Him, and through Him with the Father, is actually modelled on His own relationship with the Father?' 'I know my own and my own know me, as the Father knows me and I know the Father' (John 10:14,15). '. . . as thou, Father, art in me and I in me and I in thee. I pray that they

may also be one in us . . . that they may be one even as we are one. I in them and thou in me, that they may become perfectly one . . .' (John 17: 21–23).

The life of prayer, the life of contemplation, is simply to realise God's Presence in us. It is therefore not a special way of life reserved for those few individuals who are called to get away from the world and to dwell in the deserts. Contemplation and prayer ought to be the very breath of every disciple of Christ.[8]

The cosmic dance

It is now becoming fairly commonplace to observe, if not to participate in, dance in Christian worship. Christians are increasingly feeling that the whole of one's being, including the body, is to be presented to God in worship and adoration. The dance may be solemnly ritualistic or a free and spontaneous gambolling for joy before the Lord. Perhaps both these aspects were demonstrated in David's dancing before the ark of the covenant.[9]

But although such liturgical dancing is becoming increasingly common, there is a more ancient way of thinking of dance in adoration and worship, and that is that the whole creation is a dance, a game, a dynamic, rhythmic movement in which God himself dances through his creation. Therefore, liturgical or pentecostal dancing is but a participation in the dance of creation that is already going on.

Perhaps Christians have been afraid of the dynamic movement of God's Holy Spirit in the world of matter, as they have been afraid of using their bodies and material substances in worship. 'God is spirit, and those who worship him must worship him in spirit and in truth.' But this spiritual worship includes the totality of man's being. God pronounced matter and the material world as good–sin excepted! It is not that spiritual things are good and holy, and material things are dark and evil–that is dualism, gnosticism, Platonism. The truth, according to the Christian tradition, is that the spiritual world may be good or evil, and the material world may be good or evil. Dedication of matter and spirit to God in love is the determining factor.

There is therefore, no reason why God should not manifest himself in matter—indeed the Incarnation is the great demonstration of the goodness of matter. And this mighty act of incarnation was the initial movement of God in the redemption of the world, spirit and matter moving towards the consummation of all things when the whole cosmos is to be transfigured and spiritualised in eternal glory. Christ's transfiguration and resurrection are previews or prototypes of of this work of consummation. The transfigured physical body of Christ on the holy mountain, and the spiritual, glorified body of Christ in the resurrection, both point to the redemption of the body, and of creation as envisaged in the eschatological expectation of the early Church.[10]

During my six months of solitude on the Lleyn Peninsula during 1983–84, two of the few books I took with me were by Fritjof Capra, writing on the parallels between modern physics and mysticism, entitled *The Tao of Physics*, and *The Turning Point*. They are exciting, stimulating and demanding books, and there was enough in each chapter to keep me reading and cross-referencing. Capra sets the scene in his first book by relating his academic, scientific disciplines to an experience which became life-giving, and set him on his spiritual pilgrimage:

> Five years ago, I had a beautiful experience which set me on a road that has led to the writing of this book. I was sitting by the ocean one late summer afternoon, watching the waves rolling in and feeling the rhythm of my breathing, when I suddenly became aware of my whole environment as being engaged in a gigantic cosmic dance. Being a physicist, I knew that the sand, rocks, water and air around me were made of vibrating molecules and atoms, and that these consisted of particles which interacted with one another

by creating and destroying other particles. I knew also that the earth's atmosphere was continually bombarded by showers of 'cosmic rays', particles of high energy undergoing multiple collisions as they penetrated the air. All this was familiar to me from my research in high-energy physics, but until that moment I had only experienced it through graphs, diagrams and mathematical theories. As I sat on that beach my former experiences came to life; I 'saw' cascades of energy coming down from outer space, in which particles were created and destroyed in rhythmic pulses; I 'saw' the atoms of the elements and those of my body participating in this cosmic dance of energy; I felt its rhythm and I 'heard' its sounds . . .[11]

Notice the words he uses at the outset: '. . . watching the waves rolling in and feeling the rhythmn of my breathing . . .' It was *then* that the moment of insight came. He did not *seek* it, but was *open* to it. He did not demand it, impose himself upon it, or discover it in the sense of wresting violently the mysterious *secret* of the cosmic dance – it just 'came to him', and then he 'saw' and 'felt' and 'heard' and 'knew'. This has to do with diversity leading to unity, with suffering and with love. The end of the golden string that Capra held was his research into physics – his diversified discipline led him to the unified structure of all things, and the cosmic dance manifested the divine at the heart of all things, revealed in the multiverse rhythmic movement of the cosmos. Because I had experienced this very thing, first as a child in a basic and primitive way, I recognised what Capra was talking about – and I found it everywhere. Take these words from an essay by Alan Watts:

Ever since I can remember anything at all, the light, the smell, the sound and motion of the sea have been pure magic. Even the mere intimation of its presence – gulls flying a little way inland, the quality of light in the sky beyond hills which screen it from view, the lowing of

> foghorns in the night. If ever I have to get away from it all, and in the words of the Chinese poet 'wash all the wrongs of life from my pores', there is simply nothing better than to climb out onto a rock, and sit for hours with nothing in sight but sea and sky. Although the rhythm of the waves beats a kind of time, it is not clock or calendar time. It has no urgency. It happens to be timeless time. I know that I am listening to a rhythm which has been just the same for millions of years, and it takes me out of a world of relentlessly ticking clocks. Clocks for some reason or other always seem to be marching, and, as with armies, marching is never to anything but doom. But in the motion of waves there is no marching rhythm. It harmonizes with our very breathing. It does not count our days. Its pulse is not in the stingy spririt of measuring, of marking out how much still remains. It is the breathing of eternity . . . As a mere conception this might sound appallingly monotonous, until you come to listen to the breaking and washing of waves.[12]

And at the end of the essay he writes: 'The ocean is an environment in which the awareness of our roots can awaken, in which space so real because of the light and colour can be seen as joining things instead of separating them.'

I mentioned that I read Capra's two books during my long period of solitude. The reason I quote Watt's piece above is because I had his book as part of my bookbinding work, and his words jumped out at me.

During that six months I lived in a stone cottage at the edge of the peninsula – sea on three sides, with an exposure to earth, sea and sky. It brought together for me the objective nature of the created order with the subjectivity of my own interior life – hence the relevance of the quotes from Capra and Watts. From my own diary of that period, dated 4th February, I quote:

> I have struggled down the mountain path to the cliff-top

overlooking the Irish Sea which stretches on my right as Caernarvon Bay while on my left Bardsey Island looms out of the water at the tip of the peninsula.

I sit in a partly sheltered place, though it is impossible to play upon my recorder because of the gusts of wind. The February sun shines upon me and sparkles on the sea, reflecting the glorious whiteness of the surfing crests of the waves as they crash against the rocks below. Gusts of wind blow clouds of spray continually from the sea, and the rhythmic thudding of entry and withdrawal between the pounding sea and inlet coves reverberates like the systole and diastole of the great cosmic heartbeat re-echoed within my own body. What a place is this, and what a day!

I kept a journal and a diary at that time. My diary records my own intimate feelings of exhilaration and desolation, and sometimes of paralysis and accidie! I find it psychologically interesting that my journal often lapses into a homiletic style – I 'preach to myself', not with a view to publication but for my own immediate and later reflection. After the above paragraphs I go on, referring to the Capra and Watts quotes which I wrote into the journal:

I have quoted these passages because they are basic to me in my intuitive apprehension of the sense of 'presence' which has always been part of nature to me – as I believe it is to many who have no name for it. It has to do with awe and mystery, with wonder and terror, with gentle intimacy and wild destruction. It is because contemporary, city-dwelling, western, technological man has cut himself off from earth, sea and sky that he has lost this feeling, this awareness, this sense of primitive mystery. Exposure to technology without compensating exposure to a basic, natural environment leads men to think in terms of technological 'progress' and to act towards the natural environment without intuitive awareness, and therefore without compassion. The results are that the treatment and slaughter of animals are carried out inhumanely, the earth is raped ecologically, while in other areas, scientific research, which is part of the great involvement in the whole work of discovery, is in the pay and obedience of political powers bent on the ultimate destruction of opponents in cosmic nuclear catastrophe.

I look back upon that long period of solitude now, and I can remember that particular day clearly. I went in the strength of the two formative quotations, and spent most of the day wandering around the rocky coast, making scrappy notes, praying and singing, lying on the grass in meditation, scrambling, running, walking. This was one of many days 'living in the presence' and spending the evening or part of the next day writing it all up in my journal in shorthand – and its immediacy strikes and pursues me now as I long again for that immense solitude. Let me continue to the end of that particular section:

I begin with what is immediately before me – the sea! But what I affirm is that cosmic unity and mystery which is the fount and source of all creativity – therefore of life and love. From my earliest days I have found, in solitude, especially along the Gower coast, by the sea, during day and night, the same sense of presence that has brought me here. It is part of the great search, the openness, the awareness of the mystery which seeks me in my seeking, and finds me in my finding. It is such a mystery that I can never claim to have wholly found It, though it is as impossible to say that I have not experienced It. There is a sense in which It has found me. There is so much to be discovered about that presence which manifests Itself in all the profound and creative disciplines of the world – in academic, artistic, scientific and philosophical pursuits. Whether in a toccata and fugue of Bach or a research paper on abstruse biological research, that unitive mystery is present and makes Itself known to those who have eyes to see and ears to hear. Capra saw and felt and heard and knew in that moment of revelation, and it drew him towards a recognition of the unity of all things in the inter-relating dynamism that pervades the cosmic order. He quotes that intuitive poet, William Blake:

> To see a world in a grain of sand
> And a heaven in a wild flower,
> Hold infinity in the palm of your hand,
> And eternity in an hour,

and then says: ' . . . If the poet sees the world in a grain of sand, the modern physicist sees the world in a hadron.' How wonderful and clear is his chapter 'Interpenetration' in *The Tao of Physics* which underlines this holistic approach.

All this, understood experientially, not just intellectually, is part of the way that I have been travelling for some time, and it is the way which engages people of many religions and none, of many colours, creeds, nationalities and philosophies. It manifests that light 'which enlightens every man that comes into the world' (John 1:9) – the light of creation which is even more profoundly manifested in redemption.

Joining in the dance

There is, of course, a great danger in 'interpreting' such experience, and of imposing one's own colour and philosophy upon it. One of the great fellow-pilgrims who has been of immense help to me in this respect is Thomas Merton, the Trappist monk who blazed an amazing contemporary trail in terms of the contemplative and ecumenical life, and who died seemingly prematurely, in 1968. He urges us to join in the cosmic dance, but warns us against imposing our own meaning upon the created order. Following his lead, we must be aware of what we feel and intuit, but also see ourselves in the context of the great spiritual traditions, especially those of

Judaism and Christianity. We must be open and receptive to what the Lord reveals to us. Some of the Greek Fathers called the world the 'game of God' in which the Lord intends us to be participants – to play and dance with him in his creation. This can be experienced in all manner of ways – cross-country running, gently jogging, pedalling a bicycle as fast as one can possibly go, jumping and dancing through the waves on a sandy or rugged coast. This is participation in the dance which is the divine game, and its beauty is that it can carry us back to our childhood again. It can instil in us a new innocence, a playful gentleness, and a renewed humour and joy in creation. Merton describes it:

> What is serious to men is often very trivial in the sight of God. What in God might appear to us as 'play' is perhaps what He Himself takes most seriously. At any rate the Lord plays and diverts Himself in the garden of His creation, and if we could let go of our own obsession with what we think is the meaning of it all, we might be able to hear His call and follow Him in His mysterious, cosmic dance. We do not have to go very far to catch echoes of that game, and of that dancing. When we are alone on a starlit night; when by chance we see the migrating birds in autumn descending on a grove of junipers to rest and eat; when we see children in a moment when they are really children; when we know love in our own hearts; or when, like the Japanese poet Basho, we hear an old frog land in a quiet pond with a solitary splash – at such times the awakening, the turning inside out of all values, the 'newness', the emptiness and the purity of vision that make themselves evident, provide a glimpse of the cosmic dance.[13]

Pagan rhythm or Christian joy

Merton is careful to point out that the true cosmic dance is the reverberating grace and love of the God who created and redeemed the world. It is not an appeal to natural instinct in its alienation. It is not any kind of religious or pagan rhythm that accompanies the sensual throbbing of a pagan fertility cult. It is rather an experience of being drawn into the rhythm of the heartbeat at the centre of the cosmos. It is the rhythm and pulsation of the world which is the mind and heart of its creator and redeemer. It is heard in silence and yet in all things that glorify God in the created order. And only those who strive for purity of vision in contemplation truly participate in such a cosmic dance. The redeeming love and grace of God in Jesus Christ, applied by the power of the Holy Spirit, are the foundation upon which the contemplative life is built. The redeeming and reconciling grace of God gives rise to the restoration of the music of the dance, the celebration of creation. And whether we choose to participate in it or not, the dance goes on, for nothing can extinguish the divine light or overcome the divine grace:

> For the world and time are the dance of the Lord in emptiness. The silence of the spheres is the music of a wedding feast. The more we persist in misunderstanding the phenomena of life, the more we analyse them out into strange finalities and complex purposes of our own, the more we involve ourselves in sadness, absurdity and despair. But it does not matter much, because no despair of ours can alter the reality of things, or stain the joy of the cosmic dance which is always there. Indeed we are in the midst of it, and it is in the midst of us, for it beats in our very blood, whether we want it to or not.[14]

Sadly, in Western theology, we have often set the problems of fallenness and human sin before us in all their stark nakedness and depravity *before* the good news of the Gospel. Of course, the Gospel *is* good news to a lost and sick world, but the whole scheme of redemption is far wider and more profound in its context and implications than simply a plan of rescue. We should not begin with the fallenness of creation and the sin of man, but with the goodness and innocence depicted in the paradise story of Genesis.

The Franciscan tradition, in company with the Eastern Fathers and the ancient Celtic Church, took delight in creation, and the Franciscan friar Duns Scotus was the thirteenth-century theologian who maintained that the Incarnation would have taken place quite apart from the need for redemption. Merton puts it like this:

> The Lord God would not only love His creation as a Father, but He would enter into His creation, emptying Himself, hiding Himself, as if He were not God but a creature. Why should He do this? Because He loved His creatures, and because He could not bear that His creatures should merely adore Him as distant, remote, transcendent and all-powerful. This was not the glory that He sought.[15]

The goodness of creation as it came from the hand of God is proclaimed in the book of Genesis before the story of the Fall. Man is innocent before he is fallen, and we should affirm the original basic goodness of the created order *before* we take cognisance of the fallenness and alienation which face us in the world. The way back to that original innocence in which the *imago Dei*, the image of God is to be restored, is the way of redemption. It is to that fallenness and restoration through Christ that we now turn – from the original paradise, through paradise lost, to paradise regained. And as we take this path we should recognise our own personal and corporate experience in the pilgrimage. As we trace the theological trail, it becomes a path of inward experience. We have glimpses of our own original innocence, a sad awareness of our sinfulness and alienation, leading to the profound experience of joy in redemption.[16]

Creation is the dance of joy, and what joy has been lost to us has been regained by the redeeming love of God in Christ, so that

In Him the tribes of Adam boast
More blessings than their father lost.

Therefore the end of our redemption is restoration, the restoration of that immense joy of creation which is the inheritance of every child of Adam, for as Thomas Merton says: '. . . the fact remains that we are invited to forget ourselves on purpose, cast our awful solemnity to the winds and join in the general dance.'[17]

Notes

1 Psalm 139: 7–10
2 Ibid., vv. 23, 34.
3 Abhishiktananda (Henri Le Saux, OSB), *Prayer* (London: SPCK), p. 2.
4 Exodus 3:1–6.
5 Elizabeth Barrett Browning, 'Aurora Leigh', *The Oxford Book of English Mystical Verse*, (OUP) pp. 150ff.
6 Genesis 28:16, 17.
7 Jonah 1:1–3.
8 Abhishiktananda, op. cit., pp. 2f.
9 2 Samuel 6:14.
10 See Luke 9:28–36; Luke 24:36–43; Romans 8:18–25.
11 Fritjof Capra *The Tao of Physics* (London: Fontana/Flamingo) p. 11.
12 Alan Watts, *Cloud-Hidden, Whereabouts Unknown* (London: Jonathan Cape), pp. 15f.
13 Thomas Merton, *Seeds of Contemplation* (Wheathampstead: Anthony Clarke), p. 230.
14 Loc. cit.
15 Ibid., p. 227
16 The poetic lamentation of Wordsworth may be translated into a theological awareness of spiritual experience. See especially *The Excursion* and *Intimations of Immortality from Recollections of Early Childhood.* The whole cosmic drama is set out theologically in John Milton's *Paradise Lost* and *Paradise Regained.*
17 Merton, op. cit., p. 230.

2 Alienation: The Loss of Joy

When I first turned my mind to write about joy in Christian life and experience, I turned to the Bible, not only because it is the source of my theological thinking, in testing, confirming and challenging my experience, but also because it is the place where my own experiential thinking is clarified, corrected and given new dimensions of experimentation. And I was embarrassed by the riches of joy, exhilaration and sheer vitality found in both the Old and New Testaments.

But another fact about bringing one's thoughts and experience to the scrutiny of scripture is that it imparts an objectivity to one's thinking that is salutary, especially if there is the temptation to dig from the quarry of scripture those out-of-context quotations which suit one's argument – for even the devil can quote scripture! It is an easy matter to select quotations, themes and stories of joy, assurance and creative vitality to sustain the argument that joy is inherent in the created order. But through scripture I am faced with pain and sorrow, with complaint and anger, with disappointment, mortality, sickness, finitude and death. There are whole psalms which groan and cry to God because of the frailty of human nature, the prosperity of the wicked and the seeming negligence of God and his indifference to the tragic human situation. And these I could not ignore. In any case, they are equally part of my human experience, and to major on the themes of joy and glory without a clear recognition of the sorrows and misery of mankind would not only be lacking in objectivity, but would be downright dishonest.

A factor which is basic to this whole problem is also that finitude, mortality, pain and suffering are not only individual but corporate, and this is certainly reflected in the biblical material, as is the joy of salvation and cosmic redemption. The last chapter had to do with the Christian claim that joy and love were basic in the created order, and that there is purpose and design at the heart of things. In this chapter we shall be concerned with the loss of such joy, and the missing dimension of love in our personal and corporate lives, involving suffering and sin in all their forms. But let me begin from my own experience.

Being angry with God

The basic reason why I entered the ministry was because of a call from God – what is called a vocation. But behind that was an experience of God in creation and redemption that brought me immense joy and assurance, with the great desire to share the good news of the love of God in Christ. So, in the early days of my ordination, and in charge of a congregation of God's people in Cardiff, I expended much energy and enthusiasm, with a group of loyal and dedicated Christians who supported me wholeheartedly, during the first five years of my ministry, through joys and sorrows.

There were many formative experiences which came out of that period, but one of them was quite new to me, at least in the depths which it sounded, and in the implications it carried for my theology and practice since that time. It had to do with the problem of suffering.

Mrs Manson was an old lady in her eighties, a member of the church whom I visited regularly. I think it was more for my good than for hers, for she taught me a good deal about the love and patience of God. Whenever I visited her we would sing some of the Sankey and Moody hymns that she loved, and I always went from her refreshed in my pastoral visiting, to carry her warmth and radiance to others.

For a while she had been telling me that it was time the Lord took her 'home to be with him', and the day came when she could no longer live alone, but had to be taken into St

David's hospital in Cardiff. She was quite at peace about this, and took it all in her stride as I saw when I visited her one day. But on the way out of the ward, after visiting and praying with her, I spoke to some of the patients.

Just at the ward door there was a frail old lady in a bed with cot sides, and I bent over, took her hand and spoke gently. She saw my clerical collar and held on firmly to my arm, and said – and I can hear it now – 'Oh . . . I wasn't always like this . . .'

The effect of those few words was staggering. I had seen much pain and sorrow in the world. I had been an SRN for years, and had nursed people young and old in their pain, seen children die of leukemia and cancer, and watched at the bedsides of the terminally ill, not without much feeling and compassion. But this woman! It seemed that all the sorrow and pain, all the finitude and mortality of the world were contained in her frail person, and packed into those few words. Perhaps also it was that I was the representative of God to her at that moment, and she was crying out in the loneliness and helplessness of her desolation.

It seemed to me that I was hearing her say: 'There was a time when I was young and beautiful, independent and free. There was a time when I was in love, when I was newly married, a mother and wife. There was a time when I had health of body and clarity of mind. And now I am alone and helpless, sick and dying . . . I wasn't always like this . . .'

I don't know what I said to her. Perhaps I soothed her, prayed with her, assured her. One can do many things like that as a priest and minister while inwardly there is pain and helplessness. But what I remember is the tremendous thrust of a reaction which must have been building up over a long period of time. And it flared up in anger and complaint, and blazed against the heartlessness, the injustice, the indifference of God. 'Why have you left her like this . . . Why is she so desolate and forsaken . . . Where are you in this poor woman's life . . . ?'

The next thing I remember is leaving that hospital with all these thoughts churning around in my heart and mind, the paradoxes and contradictions of that situation with which I could not cope, and which exposed me to theological and pastoral darkness I had not allowed to surface previously.

I was about twenty-six years of age at the time, but it was a milestone of pastoral and theological experience, for out of it came some of the most profound discoveries of my life. Let me try and evaluate them.

First of all I discovered that I *could* be angry with God. I mean it was permissible. I had allowed myself to be angry. Until then I had justified the ways of God, made excuses, papered over the cracks, said 'pie in the sky when you die' instead of facing up to present inconsistencies. What I did not allow myself to do was to let my anger surface, to express it – and it needed to be acknowledged.

Secondly, not only *could* I be angry, but I *was*. I not only allowed it, but I felt it. I cried out in my anger, I complained in my bitterness – and oh, the repressed power that surfaced! There was a certain release and relief in the expression of such anger, and it was justified. How *dare* God sit indifferently in his heaven leaving that frail woman desolate in her helplessness.

Thirdly, although it took a time for this to become clear, I was angry because of my own finitude and pain – because *I* was inadequate and helpless, vulnerable and all too human. As I say, it took longer to see and acknowledge this, but the sheer relief of being able to express it was life-giving in itself.

Fourthly, I came to see quickly that I was actually re-echoing the anger and complaints of the patriarchs, prophets and psalmist:

> All the day my enemies taunt me
>   those who deride me use my name for a curse.
> For I eat ashes like bread,
>   and mingle tears with my drink,

because of thy indignation and anger;
  for thou hast taken me up and thrown me away.
My days are like an evening shadow;
  I wither away like grass[1]

The fact is that my theology had not been biblical enough. I had varnished over those deep dimensions of doubt, frustration, anger and bewilderment that threatened to overwhelm the prophetic biblical characters with whom I identified in other ways. Even my christology was defective enough not to allow Jesus to mean what he said when he cried out in mortal anguish: 'My God, my God, why have you forsaken me?' I had constructed a Catholic and Reformed theology that explained away that cry of dereliction, exhausting its meaning in an objective theory of the atonement. I do not deny such objective value in the atoning work of Christ, but what I did *not* do was to allow Jesus really to experience the dereliction in his humanity, in the way it is clearly expressed.

These things seem to be negative, but they yielded the most fruitful results, and they drove me into intuitive, compassionate and theological thinking which enables me to make positive affirmations which were rooted in real human experience, such as the following:

First, I had allowed myself to be totally identified with this woman's pain. In the medical and religious world I had learned to be objective – for how could one truly serve another unless one kept one's distance, a healthy objectivity, a professional distance? Of course, there is a certain sense in this – one cannot burst into tears at every funeral when one has to conduct a wedding later that day! But such professional distance was not a mark of Jesus' ministry. I am being somewhat hard on myself at this point, because there were times when I wept with patients and penitents, but there were also times when I maintained an objective distance. From this time, I allowed myself to weep over my own pains, to share them, to be vulnerable myself. And doing that enabled me to enter into the pains of others. And into their joys too.

Secondly, I learned over a period of weeks and months that my anger was not my own. It was an expression of anger on behalf of others. It was a manifestation of the legitimate human response of humankind to the inequality, injustice and cruelty of the world. It was directed against God because where else could I direct it? I was no humanist, no atheist, no existentialist – I was a committed Christian! I felt then that I was acting *for and on behalf of* my own kind, my own species, my own humanity, crying out for justice, for compassion, for love, for healing, and perhaps for forgiveness, though that was not part of it initially.

Thirdly, I learned the greatest, the most profound thing – that it was not I who was crying and shouting and blaming – it was God himself within me. I mean it was, in a paradoxical sense, the God within crying to the God above. I remember at the time being critical of one of the songs of Sydney Carter, until I suddenly realised what it was saying:

It's God they ought to crucify
Instead of you and me
I said to the Carpenter
When hanging on the tree.

The fact is that in some strange way God was in the dock, sentenced by a victimised humanity, and it was God himself who ascended the Cross, *for and on behalf of his own kind*, and bore the pain, the suffering, the infinite sorrows which brought redemption. Of course I had assented to theories of atonement previously – I was most Evangelical and Catholic in my evaluation of the Cross. But then and there, out of that experience, I understood in a far deeper way that Jesus was the man of sorrows, the despised and rejected, who bore away the sins of the world.

And this led to a complete reversal of mood – from anger to

tears, from complaint to penitence and sorrow and anguish and love. And out of this was born a new compassion. For I realised, not immediately, but over the weeks and months following, that God himself was suffering in the grief and pain of the world. It was not that some objective theological transaction had taken place two thousand years ago, but that the heart of God *always* suffered, the tears of God always fell, the blood of God was eternally shed for the sins and the sorrows of the world. It is simply expressed in the children's hymn:

> I sometimes think about his cross
> And shut my eyes and try to see
> The cruel nails, and crown of thorns,
> And Jesus crucified for me.
>
> But even could I see him die,
> I could but see a little part
> Of that great love which like a fire
> Is always burning in his heart.

If that was true, then the compassion of God overflowed in love towards suffering humanity, and it was expressed primarily in the incarnate life of our Lord Jesus, for as St Matthew says about the healing ministry of Jesus, quoting the prophet Isaiah: 'He took our infirmities and bore our diseases.'[2] In his life, death and resurrection, Jesus made himself available to human need in all its manifestations. It meant that I could come to him in all my own human vulnerability as a sinner first, and then as a minister of God in the prophetic ministry, receiving his healing and compassion, and become a channel of his healing power to other lives.

And this is the point at which it led to joy. Not then and there to a kind of leaping and dancing and praising God; not then to some ecstatic or charismatic outburst; but to a quiet but profound joy that sustained my ministry in a new way, because God's joy and God's tears are inextricably united in his love.

Feeling the pain of the world

Sometimes when I preach, after having carefully prepared, I throw the notes away and preach spontaneously. This is what has happened in this chapter. I had not intended to expound that experience so fully because I have gone off the point! But I must let it stand because I believe that it is what the Lord intends. Instead of keeping to the point of the *loss* of joy in that poor woman's life, I have gone on to show the positive fruits of that experience in my own life and ministry. But you see the point – there *was* a loss of joy, and *she* may well have died in loneliness, though I can believe that if I got so much from the experience, she must have found help too.

I can pick up the threads of my theme from that story. It seems that right there I was zooming in to the pain of the world. That story, lifted from my early pastoral experience, is one which is a microcosm, a reflection of the whole of human pain. There is a solidarity inherent in our humanity, we belong to one another, and if humanity is one tree, we are all limbs, branches and leaves growing from it. This means that there is a mutual participation in joy and sorrow. If God is our home, our true Love, from whom we come and to whom we go – if God is the source and root of our being in whom we live, move and exist – and if we are cut off from him – then there is a solidarity in our misery, a sympathy and compassion in our pain. Of course, this is too much to bear, and we employ many means of numbing our sensitivity to such pain. But if we are open and loving in orientation, then we become sharers, and even bearers, of the sadness of our poor and fallen humanity.

The book of Genesis not only records the goodness and innocence of creation as it came from the hand of God, but goes on to record the awful cosmic rupture that was brought about by man's sin, producing disorder and alienation, not only between the Creator and the creature, and between man and the created order, but also betwen man and man. Solidarity gave way to division, and perversely, there emerged a solidarity of misery as a result of such alienating division within man's soul. Man did not totally lose his power, but he lost his power for uncorrupted good, and worked havoc upon the created order, now so evident in the ecological pollution we all witness, and the threatening mushroom cloud that imprinted itself upon our common mind on 6th August 1945 – a reversal of the Transfiguration which the Church celebrates on that day.

The alienation is corporate as well as personal It affects the relations between nations as well as between families, and reveals disintegration and distraction within the heart of man himself. The archetypal Adam, being separated from God, blames and misunderstands Eve; their two sons are out of step with each other, and Cain in murdering Abel is branded with the mark of exile and loneliness. And so it goes on.

Later in Genesis, as the story of Joseph unfolds, we discover that the early cosmic and earthly dreams of the young man are disrupted and betrayed by alienation and deceit among his own brothers. Pretence and separation spin out the years of exile and bereavement, and it is only by the hidden providential love of God that reconciliation takes place, and pattern and meaning are woven into the cloth which seems to have been ruined by sin.[3]

The disorder of human existence

In his book *The Principles of Christian Theology*[4] John Macquarrie looks at the phenomenon of human existence as it reveals itself, enedeavouring to draw out of our common experience something of the reality of the disorder that is part of our personal and corporate life. He sees such disorder exemplified in five sets of polarities which indicate the loss of healthy equilibrium and balance. Reference to such polarities are a further indication of loss of joy in human life, and the method which John Macquarrie employs in this early section of his theological system is to proceed with an observation of the human situation apart from divine revelation.

He first draws attention to the poles of *possibility and facticity* in human existence. Man is filled with the yearning of the possible, but bound by the limitations of what he can actually accomplish. He is hemmed in, imprisoned, beset by the limitations which come from his environment, his heredity, his intelligence, race and temperament, compounded by the limits of his power and knowledge and of the particular society in which he lives. What is *possible* is so limited by the facts of his nature and existence that real tensions are experienced.

Secondly, Macquarrie points out the related polarity between *rationality and irrationality*. Man seems, as a rational animal, to be able to judge, discriminate, sift and interpret. Yet this rationality which marks out as human is as qualified as his freedom. Freud has shown us how our lives are frequently ruled by dark, irrational forces. We do not really understand our own motives, and our ignorance is revealed in the fact that we are under irrational pressures. We long for truth, and at the same time move in realms of untruth, error and deception. Man's rationality often works toward disruption, disintegration and destruction.

Another polarity is the opposition between *responsibility and impotence*. We have a sense of conscience, of ought, of responsive action calling for positive and compassionate decision. There is a certain interior self-awareness, but the voice of such an awareness may sound clear, while the ability to carry out its implications is weak to the point of impotence. 'I ought' therefore does not often imply 'I can', rather the opposite. As Macquarrie points out, there are existentialists like Jean-Paul Sartre who would claim that man's existence is simply self-contradictory, and that man is a useless passion, making nonsense of his aspirations and potentialities. This seems to be confirmed in the enshrouding darkness of death which, apart from the revelation of the Gospel, is the end of all, indicating a triumph of finitude and negativity over any sparks of positive and affirmative being in human existence. It is extremely difficult for us to accept that our existence is so absurd and futile – that we are thrown into a meaningless existence of contradiction, ending in death. The existentialist philosophers themselves endeavour to get beyond this, often with great courage in the face of it all.

This brings us to another aspect of vulnerable human existence, the polarity of *anxiety and hope*. Because of the foregoing polarities, it is clear why we are beset by anxiety. The threat of absurdity and negativity is sufficient to bring us into such a state. It is not merely an emotional mood which merely reflects subjective considerations, but a considered consequence of our observations. Of course, an emotional state is involved, and a certain hope is present. The temptation for the Christian is to run away from such dark disclosure of human existence, taking refuge in the hope disclosed in the Gospel. It is possible to use the Gospel as an opiate when faced with humanity's suffering and meaninglessness in the context of the holocaust of ten million people under Stalinist terror, or six million Jews under the regime of Hitler. As Macquarrie points out, hope and anxiety have seen many oscillations in the twentieth century, from a brash, unthinking optimism to an apolalyptic despair.

The final polarity that Macquarrie discussed is that between *individuality and community*. Here again, acute tension is often experienced. The importance of privacy, individuality and autonomy and the demands of social and political units, especially in an increasingly bureaucratic society, are often contradictory. And where totalitarian regimes operate, this may lead to imprisonment, torture, and death. The privacy and autonomy of the individual is to be respected and preserved, his uniqueness is to be recognised and protected. But the need for community and the demands of social and political policy set up destructive tensions. Community demands may be the frustration of individual fulfilment and realisation. If individuals tend to disrupt the community by self-seeking, societies also tend to oppress individuals through collective egoism and institutional injustice.

The emphasis is different at different times and in differing individuals. Individual salvation and corporate wholeness are equally important and the relationship is often complex, but they have significant parallels, such as the supreme importance of the death of an individual and the apocalyptic situation of the possibility of the end of all mankind. As Macquarrie points out, the personal-corporate boundaries are sometimes blurred in the Bible. In Abraham in the Old Testament, and in Christ in the New, sometimes the individual is intended and sometimes the community – one can be 'in Abraham' or 'in Christ'.

Macquarrie goes on to delineate the *disorder of existence*, giving, first of all, a philosophical analysis, and then a theological one. His method in diagnosing and evaluating, outside faith and within faith, is invaluable. In taking the phenomenon of human existence as it stands, totally seriously, it becomes clear that in a secular and a spiritual sense, there is a tremendous lack or loss of joy in human life.

I want to show, in the next chapter, the recovery of joy in redemption, and the immense difference to human life when the Holy Spirit of Joy comes to dwell in the human heart. But here we face the reality of lack and loss of joy in the fallenness of our human condition. We may read the thanksgiving of an optimistic nineteenth-century theologian in the following prayer, but its implications seem to fall like a shadow within the words of thanksgiving:

God, who created me
Nimble and light of limb,
In three elements free,
To run, to ride, to swim;

Not when the sense is dim,
But now from the heart of joy,
I would remember him:
Take the thanks of a boy.

Relationships

At some time or another, and perhaps frequently, we experience the breakdown of existing human relationships. We are unable to initiate or sustain warmth, creativity and positive harmony because of an alienating process which we find arising within ourselves or others. Often this does not seem to be under our control, and we cannot seem to put the matter right or make at-one-ment.

Sometimes it is clear where the fault lies and by mutual openness, forgiveness, understanding and humour, we can break through to a new creative flow of compassion and love, or at least to mutual and good-humoured tolerance. Sometimes the fault is in the other person and he will not listen, look, examine or even doubt his rightness. And sometimes the fault is in us, and we will not allow ourselves the humility of re-examination and confession. But sometimes it seems there is no obvious solution to the breakdown, and though there is a certain preparedness on both sides, yet still the relationship cannot be reconstituted as it was.

Perhaps, too, we have been either the victim or perpetrator of the kind of breakdown which William Blake portrays in his poem *The Poison Tree*:

I was angry with my friend,
I told my wrath, my wrath did end;
I was angry with my foe,
I told it not, my wrath did grow.

And I watered it with fears,
Night and morning with my tears;
And I sunnéd it with smiles,
And with soft, deceitful wiles.

And it grew both day and night,
Till it bore an apple bright,
And my foe beheld it shine
And he knew that it was mine,

And into my garden stole
When the night had veiled the pole:
In the morning, glad, I see
My foe outstretched beneath the tree.

The vicious circle of sin seems to draw others into the web and whirlpool of its embrace, and the conception-birth-maturity cycle illustrates the terrible recurring pattern: '... After desire has conceived, it gives birth to sin; and sin, when it is full-grown, gives birth to death.'[5]

The perplexing, alienating pattern is expounded in the Adam story in the Epistle to the Romans,[6] but here, as in the Genesis stories, there is always the light of hope, the promise of redemption, the revelation of the Last Adam who reverses the consequences of the Fall, as the Fall reversed the blessings of paradise. As John Henry Newman has it;

O loving wisdom of our God!
When all was sin and shame,
A second Adam to the fight
And to the rescue came.

The whole cosmos, including and especially man himself, feels the pain and disorder of the world. The creative energies of musicians, writers and poets beat out the rhythm of sadness, and they reverberate in the still, sad music of humanity. The monastery in which I live is dedicated to St Mary at the Cross, and it is in her heart that the sorrows of the world may be concentrated. She stood there, desolate and alone, gazing upon the Man of Sorrows who was her own dear Son. Part of our task as we daily offer prayer and sacrament in this place is to enter more profoundly into the pain and sorrow of the world, in order that the Man of Sorrows himself may take, heal and transform it from pain to glory:

O that blessed one, grief-laden,
Blessed Mother, blessed maiden,
  Mother of the all-holy one;
O that silent, ceaseless mourning,
O those dim eyes, never turning
  From that wondrous, suffering Son.

Who on Christ's dear Mother gazing,
In her trouble so amazing,
  Born of woman, would not weep?
Who on Christ's dear Mother thinking,
Such a cup of sorrow drinking,
  Would not share her sorrow deep?

In company with Mary at the Cross, we offer the world's pain and alienation to the Saviour Christ, and believe that in our compassion and prayers the world's healing continues. The loss of joy is redeemed only as we enter into the implications of the world's darkness, for then there is an ecstasy of joy. This is what is meant by one of the Desert Father stories:

> Abba Isaac said; 'Once I was sitting with Abba Poemen, and I saw that he was in an ecstasy; and I used to speak very openly with him, I made a prostration before him and asked him, "Tell me, where were you?" And he did not want to tell me. But when I pressed him, he replied: "My thoughts were with St Mary the Mother of God, as she stood and wept at the Cross of the Saviour; and I wish that I could always weep as much as she wept then."

Notes

1 Psalm 102:8–11.
2 Matthew 8:17, quoting Isaiah 53:4

3 See Genesis chapters 37 to 50
4 John Macquarrie, *The Principles of Christian Theology* (London: SCM)
5 James 1:15
6 Romans 5:12–7:25; See also the Adam-Christ parallel in 1 Corinthians 15:45, 57.

3 Redemption: The Recovery of Joy

Paradise Lost and Regained

One cold, clear December day, with the bright sunshine bathing the countryside of Dorset and Somerset, I climbed up the Batcombe Ridge on a free afternoon from our Dorset Friary. It is a climb which I always associate with periods of solitude and prayer in the hut which was hidden among the hillside of trees a mile or two along the Ridge. The day was bracing, I was full of natural exuberance and spiritual joy. At such times I seek solitude so that I can be noisily full of praise, moving into the silence of wonder and adoration.

I got to the top of the Ridge beautifully puffed and out of breath, and lay down on my back, gazing into the wide expanse of blue, with white clouds scudding across my line of vision. This was an ideal day, time and place for simply allowing the Lord to take me where he wanted me – to abandon myself into his love, and let praise and worship flow where it would. The glorious thing about a spirituality which allows and encourages such spontaneity is that the more I 'let it be', the more I experience the different and varying manifestations of the Lord's way with me. There are times when he plays a game with me – almost tossing me up in the air and catching me again – or playing hide-and-seek in causing his radiance to shine through the clouds, filter through the trees, burst from the earth, spring in the turf or come showering down in rain or blow in the wind.

But there are other times when he changes the mood gently or suddenly. It may begin with the glory of such a day as I have described and then suddenly I am plunged into the pain and sorrow of a world shot through with pain and suffering.

And this leads me to periods of groaning and intercession for those who are shut away from such natural glory, or writing in the agony of torture, hunger or drought. I don't dictate what the Lord does, or the way he takes me.

However, on this day I began to sing – and to sing two hymns, both metrically the same, sung to the same tune, but illustrating both the dance of creation's exuberance, and the sorrow and deeper joy of redemption's cost. First it was:

Just as I am, young, strong and free,
To be the best that I can be
For truth, and righteousness, and Thee,
  Lord of my life, I come.

In the glad morning of my day,
My life to give, my vows to pay,
With no reserve and no delay,
  With all my heart I come.[1]

That's a fine hymn and on that day in Dorset it expressed so much of the glory, the exuberance, the vitality, the sheer joy of living that I felt – climbing, running, dancing, 'leaping for joy' in the presence of the Lord. But there was also an underlying vein of penitence and sadness which was as much a part of my experience. Certainly I had to use a bit of poetic licence to sing 'young, strong and free', and 'in the glad morning of my day', but I *felt* like that then, and still do (mostly!).

But I also know that I am *not* young and strong as I was, and that I am *not* in the glad morning of my day. And more than that – not only do I feel my own finitude, mortality and the sad yearning that comes in middle life, but I have been shabby, unfaithful, critical, hypocritical and downright sinful in my life before God and other people. I have grieved the heart of God and hurt relationships with others. I am ashamed and I am penitent. And I cannot accept the 'glad morning' without the rest of it. And so I began to sing the second hymn:

Just as I am – poor, wretched, blind;
Sight, riches, healing of the mind,
Yea, all I need, in Thee to find,
O Lamb of God, I come.

Just as I am – Thou wilt receive,
Wilt welcome, pardon, cleanse, relieve:
Because Thy promise I believe,
O Lamb of God, I come.

The wonder of that day was that I could rejoice, be penitent and rejoice again. It was paradise, paradise lost and paradise regained – all in one afternoon! And it was felt, lived experienced. And although sorrow was the dark backcloth, yet joy contributed the glorious colours which made the canvas live and sparkle with meaning. And that is not the end of the story, as we shall go on to see. But at least I could break out into the singing of the last stanzas of the latter hymn – in biblical fashion, because there is no joy in scripture without reference to eschatology – the coming kingdom and glory of our Lord Jesus Christ, when he shall reign as prince of peace and cosmic Lord of all:

Just as I am – Thy love unknown
Has broken every barrier down;
Now to be Thine, yea, Thine alone,
O Lamb of God, I come.

Just as I am – of that free love
The breadth, length, depth, and height to prove,
Here for a season, then above,
O Lamb of God, I come.

I came down from that afternoon, having used my body, mind and spirit – all the faculties of sight, sound, smell and touch – having tasted the goodness and pain of creation and redemption in communion with the Lamb of God who was crucified upon Calvary and worshipped in the Apocalypse.[3] Because of such a time of solitude, reflection and worship I was more able to enter into the life of a busy friary, catering for the needs of brothers, professed and novices, of members of the friary family, people in care, wayfarers and guests, and find reflected in them the very glory and pain expressed in those two hymns.

Nature and Grace

The experience of joy in redemption is centred in the cross of Jesus, and though I may wax eloquent at times about the joy and glory of creation, I am well aware that my sense of exhilaration in the created order is countered by another's pain and grief at 'nature red in tooth and claw'. There is a buoyancy, a physical and emotional delight, a clean stimulation of the senses when I run or swim or ride – when I plunge into the foam-crested waves or roll on the springy turf of a verdant hillside with a panorama of natural beauty rolling out below me. But what when I am bereaved, suffering, lonely or broken in heart?

My long periods of solitude, first of all in the soft loveliness of Dorset in spring and summer, and secondly in the wild bleakness and bare splendour of autumn and winter in the Lleyn Peninsula, have exposed me to, and immersed me in, a theology of nature, of the cyclic seasons, of birth, death and resurrection. And I share meditative and contemplative experience with all men of all ages throughout the world who have ever been exposed and immersed in the beauty and desolation of natural solitude. The descriptive philosophies of such experience may vary in colour and tone, in language and thought-form, according to birth, training, period, philosophy or religion – but the divine mystery shining through the natural phenomena is at the heart of such communication. I share so much with so many, and recognise in ancient writings, especially of Eastern contemplative and mystical traditions, a similar experience to mine. But this is not enough! I need an experience of redemption, of forgiveness, of grace and reconciliation. It is not enough to say:

> How sweet the name of *nature* sounds
> In a believer's ear;
> It soothes his sorrows, heals his wounds,
> And drives away his fear.

No! Only *Jesus* can do that! I have known the stirrings of mystical experience from a child. I was aware of the strange movement of creative and cosmic life within me when in my loneliness, often in late evening, I would walk by the sea, along the sand or on the cliff path of the Gower Peninsula. The constant movement of the sea, sometimes thudding rhythmically and gently, lapping against the rocks, and sometimes heaving and swelling in potentially destructive power, were often the context of such meditative walks. When this was combined with a starry night, the broad expanse of wide sky, and the pale reflection of waxing or waning moon upon the water, you can imagine how my young heart was moved and stirred. But above and beyond and deeper than all this was my *response* to it, in all those deep places of feeling, of love, of creativity, of inspiration. I could not have written or talked like this of it then, but it was all there in embryo. It seems to me that what I do now is to allow my infancy and childhood to unfold themselves within me, and to respond to such unfolding, participating as I do in the present reality of the divine mystery which continues to move in me to this day. I feel like Angelus Silesius:

> Because the Godhead was
> In childhood shown to me
> To Godhead and to childhood
> I am drawn equally.

The point I am making is that I needed the revelation and experience of redemption to bring together nature and grace, fallenness and reconciliation. Again, Angelus Silesius expresses it clearly:

> Though Christ in Bethlehem
> A thousand times be born,
> If he's not born in thee
> Thy soul remains forlorn.

The experience of my own heart, even in childhood, included the knowledge of the fallenness of nature and the bitterness and violence that arose between children, let alone men and women, in the area of human relationships. I realised that nature, too, revealed a destructive element. Beneath the vision of glory and design, of rhythm and meaning reflected in the cosmic cycle, there were predators and victims, one species preying upon another. The Garden of Eden was overrun with thorns and brambles, although the luminosity of the divine Presence was never wholly withdrawn. I still remember as a child musing upon the darkness and loneliness within, reflecting upon the chill winters of solitary wanderings, and knowing moments of strange fear even on clear sunny days.

What I needed was a vision and experience of redemption, forgiveness and reconciliation in myself and the world. And that is what came about! At twelve years of age, a specific experience and encounter with the Christ of faith took place after a missionary service. Well I remember first reading an anonymous hymn which I have never heard sung, but which I immediately claimed as mine:

> I sought the Lord, and afterwards I knew
> He moved my soul to seek Him, seeking me;
> It was not I that found, O Saviour true;
> No, I was found of thee.

Thou didst reach forth Thy hand and mine enfold;
I walked and sank not on the storm-vexed sea;
'Twas not so much that I on Thee took hold
As Thou, dear Lord, on me.

I find, I walk, I love, but O the whole
Of love is but my answer, Lord, to Thee!
For Thou wert long before-hand with my soul;
Always Thou lovedst me.

The whole meaning of Jesus – his incarnation, life of compassion, death on the cross and resurrection – was the revelation and work of reconciliation. It was the movement of the divine Love towards creation – grace redeeming and elevating nature so that such Love may shine luminously through the whole created order, ultimately redeeming and transfiguring it in the second coming of Christ, so that God may be all in all.

These were the notes I needed to hear, contributing to the harmony of Love which sounded the music of reconciliation. I needed to know, by revelation and experience, that Love was at the heart of all things. I needed confirmation of my intuition that the mystery at the heart of creation was of a piece with the redeeming revelation of Love in the Gospel. In short, I longed to be able to affirm that the divine Love was at the heart of all things and would ultimately be victorious.

Natural theology cannot stand alone. To enter into the joy of natural beauty, order and creativity there has to be the potential and the experience of suffering. Part of those precious childhood memories was the interior reasoning and response set up by the strange mystery of the world. I could not talk theology or think philosophically, but I could feel and intuit the powerful, pervading cosmic life-force that breathed in the winds, moved in the heave and swell of the sea, died and rose in the rising and setting of the sun, and that moved me sometimes to tears and sometimes to emotional and physical ecstasy. But that is not the whole truth. The very fact that I had a childlike sensitivity to beauty meant that I became compassionately aware of sadness. In fact, the colour and smell of autumn's sadness stimulated in me a spiritual yearning for immortality – after all, I was an October child. It was as if my own finitude was reflected in the dying of things, creating a soul-hunger in which the seeds of eternity sent down roots into my very being. This seemed to me to be more important an experience than the stirring of new life in spring or the blossoming of radiant beauty in high summer.

It was only when I entered into a saving knowledge of the Jesus of Calvary that I could more fully understand the pain and glory of God in nature. Poetry says it better than prose in the words of Joseph Plunkett:

> I see his blood upon the rose
> And in the stars the glory of his eyes;
> His body gleams amid eternal snows,
> His tears fall from the skies.
>
> I see his face in every flower;
> The thunder and the singing of the birds
> Are but his voice, and carven by his power
> Rocks are his written words.
>
> All pathways by his feet are worn,
> His strong heart stirs the ever-beating sea,
> His crown of thorns is twined with every thorn,
> His cross is every tree.

If his cross is every tree there is a universality about the experience that finds God in nature and in redemption. It participates both in joy and sorrow, and there is a complementarity that unites both in the maturing experience of redeeming love.

The Joy of the Cross

We cannot understand the darkness and terror of the cross to Jesus. The Garden of Gethsemane is an indication of the profound depths of spiritual agony which our Lord endured in anticipation of the bleak hill of Golgotha, the place of the skull. The strange cry of dereliction sounds through the desolate darkness and down through the ages, re-echoed in every human cry of pain: 'My God, my God, why have you forsaken me?' The sun is veiled and the earth quakes at that cry, and nature shudders at the sound. This reveals to us the manner in which God himself is involved in the pain and sorrow of our humanity, not merely having compassion from afar, but incarnating himself in human flesh in order that he might descend into the depths of human sin, pain and alienation.

But there is another side to it. Looking back on the path that Jesus trod, the theology of the Epistle to the Hebrews portrays him as entering into the joy of the redeemed even as he descended into the abyss of darkness and death. He not only endured the cross, but gloried in it;

> Jesus the pioneer and perfecter of our faith, who for the joy that was set before him, endured the cross, despising the shame, and is seated at the right hand of the throne of God.

This was no superficial or transient joy for the Man of Sorrows who was acquainted with grief. But it was the joy of consummation – the prodigal son had returned to the Father, the wandering sheep was brought back to the true fold by the Good Shepherd. Both the cry of dereliction and the sound of rejoicing are encapsulated in the old gospel hymn:

> None of the ransomed ever knew
> How deep were the waters crossed;
> Nor how dark was the night that the Lord passed through,
> 'Ere He found His sheep that was lost;
> Out in the desert He heard its cry,
> Sick and helpless and ready to die.

And all through the mountains, thunder-riven,
And up from the rocky steep,
There rose a cry to the gate of heaven,
'Rejoice, I have found my sheep!'
And the angels echoed around the throne,
'Rejoice, for the Lord brings back His own.'

The very word *redemption*, *lutreo*, was used of the buying back of the life of a slave in the market place, and one can imagine the sheer joy of redemption in the experience of a slave thus liberated. And yet some of the most beautiful negro spiritual songs celebrating the redeeming power of the cross were born out of the suffering of the old American slave trade. The themes of world-weariness, longing for heaven and rest, total trust and dependence on God and the wonder of Calvary were all present in the old plantation songs and hymns. The Egypt-land of servitude and suffering gave way to the Canaan-land flowing with milk and honey, and the redeemer Moses was a prototype of the Saviour Jesus who led the poor slaves into the promised land of forgiveness and freedom on earth, while Elijah's sweet chariot swung low to carry the pilgrims into the heavenly Canaan of Glory. The pathos, heaviness and ecstatic joys of pilgrims going home are re-echoed in these spirituals interpreted by black voices from a black soul.

A theology which works

In this chapter I have spoken of a theology of creation and a theology of redemption. They are far from being incompatible – they are integral to one another. Indeed when they are held in isolation they can become heresy. A theology of creation can become the kind of pantheism that *identifies* God with his creation, or the kind of deism in which God creates and then distances himself from intimate relationship with his creatures, or the kind of nature-mysticism which is found in that beautiful but sad book *The Story of my Heart*, by Richard Jeffries. In him can be felt the kind of nature melancholy that is touched by autumnal beauty but cannot vibrate with resurrection hope in the coming spring.

But a theology of redemption and grace which ignores the dimension of creation can neglect or misunderstand the reality of the human dimension, interpreting the breaking-in of God as something so entirely new as to be alien to human hopes and longings planted in the created order and in the human heart.

I make this point because the recovery of joy in redemption restores lost and alienated man not only to the love of God manifested in the cross, but to the heartbeat of God in the natural order, which yearns and groans together in all its parts, awaiting the fulness of our redemption in the consummation of all things.

There is immense joy in the assurance of sins forgiven and reconciliation with God through the redeeming work of Christ. And there is immense joy in the experienced awareness of God in all the beauty, harmony and balance of the created world. Yet our salvation is not yet complete – fulness of joy is not yet, and one of the marks of a redeemed humanity in its present state is the sense of incompleteness and yearning for full redemption. I think I feel this most when offering praise and adoration to God for the beauty of creation and redemption. It is illustrated in the German hymn, *Schönster Herr Jesu*:

Fairest Lord Jesus,
Lord of all creation,
Jesus of God and Mary the Son;
You will I cherish,
You will I honour,
You are my soul's delight and crown.

Fair are the meadows,
Fairer still in the woodlands,
Robed in the verdure and bloom of Spring.
Jesus is fairer,
Jesus is purer,
He makes the saddest heart to sing.

Fair are the flowers
Fairer still the sons of men
In all the freshness of youth arrayed;
Yet is their beauty
Fading and fleeting;
My Jesus, yours will never fade.

All fairest beauty
Earthly and heavenly,
Wondrously, Jesus, in you is found;
None can be nearer,
Fairer or dearer,
Than you, my Saviour, to me bound.

Notes

1 *Just as I am*, by Marianne Farningham (1834–1909), *Hymns of Faith* 477 (London: Scripture Union).
2 *Just as I am*, by Charlotte Elliott (1789–1871), *Hymns of Faith* 283.
3 Luke 23; 32,33.
4 Hebrews 12:2.

4 Triune Love: The Source of Joy

The Joy of God

When people ask me to talk about prayer, I try to discover whether they want some help with practical methods, aids, techniques, liturgical and charismatic forms of prayer – or whether they want to learn of the essence of prayer itself. It is comparatively easy to teach techniques, aids and forms, but quite another thing to enter into the profound reality of prayer, for prayer is a gift. It is often better to do without aids and forms if the Holy Spirit visits you with a gift or burden of prayer and love, for it will find its own level and its own outlet in such a case.

So it is with God. There are numerous liturgical, philosophical and ethical approaches to theological study, and there are whole systems of dogmatic theology which demand stringent discipline and application, which yield intellectual and aesthetic satisfaction to the student. But none of this need involve a living experience of God. That is of another order, though it ought not to be divorced from application of mind and heart. Thomas Merton once commented that you cannot say 'all theology is straw' with Thomas Aquinas until and unless you are prepared to investigate the theological system which demanded Aquinas's disciplined mind!

So in this chapter I am not concerned to communicate the content of any theological system, nor to exhort the reader to a study of the original languages, profitable though that would be; nor yet to pursue a philosophical study of trinitarian doctrine. But I am concerned to communicate something of the reality of the dynamic joy and love that comes from a felt participation in the life of the Holy Trinity. And that is really doing theology!

There is a stupendous claim made in the second letter of Peter which is consonant with the rest of the New Testament – that we are 'partakers of the divine nature'.[1] We share the very life of God. And one of the chief manifestations of that life is joy. If you take up a concordance and trace the various expressions of lively joy, it will become clear that they all have their source in God himself It is not simply that there is a certain joy in recognising his creative and redemptive claim upon human life, nor merely that there is a simply human joy in adoration and worship – but that human joy which is roooted in righteousness and compassion, and often overflows in an infusion of spiritual inebriation, finds God as its very source. Joy is the upsurge and overflow of the divine life in nature and in human experience.

At creation we are told that the morning stars sang together and all the sons of God shouted for sheer joy, and in the redemption of a single sinner we are assured that there is joy in the presence of the angels.[2] For that reason we are able with joy to draw water from the wells of salvation, for the Bible attributes joy to the Father, the Son and the Holy Spirit.[3]

Scriptures of the Old and New Testaments display an embarrassing richness of joyful testimony, directly and indirectly bearing witness to the joy which overflows from the bounty of the Godhead, streaming from the mountains of creation and the springs of redemption. This is confirmation of the experience of joy which may be directly perceived in creation, and is basic to the created order, in contrast to the melancholy sadness which is the temporary and intermediate state of our present existence. The promise is that though weeping may endure for a night, joy comes in the morning, and that though sowing may be in tears and hope, the harvest will be fulfilment and consummation in joy.[4]

The primacy of joy

If the manifestation of joy is grounded in God, and is basic to the dynamic life and love of the Holy Trinity, that gives joy the primacy over melancholy, misery, and all the human sadness and pain that lead to despair. This is the theological basis upon which one can assure the man who is depressed that there are objective reasons why he should not believe that despair is proper to his human nature or need enslave him.

I do not mean there is any slick or easy way out of depressive and psychic illness. But there is need for an affirmation of the primacy of joy, life and light in a world in which we live so close to the abyss of personal and corporate despair and catastrophe. If psychic health is the basic and normal condition, then psychic sickness and disintegration is astray from the norm. If the native condition of the human psyche is joy, then misery and depression can be thought of as invasive, parasitic and abnormal. Therefore there is hope for those who are alienated, who have deviated from the norm, who are oppressed by sickness or circumstances; for at the root of creation is joy, its source is God, and its manifestation is redemption, life and wholeness.

It may be a long haul from depressive illness and psychological breakdown to a renewal and restoration of health, but at least there can be a clear and affirmative attitude if you believe that there is an objective wholeness, sanity and joy at the heart of things. Perhaps it is because of the lack of such assurance on the primacy of joy and the objectivity of love in our society that our psychiatric institutions as well as our prisons are bursting at the seams. How sad it is that those whose behaviour does not measure up to that required in our sophisticated society cause the rest of us such embarrassment that we would prefer such people to be out of sight and therefore out of mind. Over the last decade or so there are diversified alternative approaches so that such people can be cared for and contained within our society—that is surely better for them and for us.

One interesting thing is that though joy may be absent from depressive illness, there is an abundance of joy in many 'patients' who suffer from Downes' syndrome or are thought to be mentally retarded, sub-normal or handicapped. In a strange way this seems to emphasise the point I am making–there is a natural upsurge of joy, playfulness and often mischievous glee in such a child or adult, often accompanied by chuckling and dancing, and an uninhibited response to music. This seems to me to be in the nature of spontaneous and natural response where there is no societal inhibition. When the prophetic spirit took hold of some of God's people in the Old Testament they began to behave in ways which were not acceptable to some of Moses' men, and they asked him to restrain them, but his answer was plain; 'Would that all the Lord's people were prophets, that the Lord would put his spirit upon them!'[5] The lesson I am suggesting we may learn is that if we could rediscover the childlike simplicity of the Gospel, and lose some of our sophisticated formal attitudes and respectability, we might glimpse again the childlikeness of the way of Christ as some of the early Franciscans experienced it.

There is a quite dotty story told in *The Little Flowers of St Francis*. Francis and Masseo came to a crossroads between Florence, Siena and Arezzo, not knowing which way the Lord would have them go. So Francis spun Masseo around like a little child until he was completely dizzy, and suddenly commanded him to stop. He stopped–and was facing Siena, and that was the way Francis felt God undoubtedly wanted them to go!

When Masseo thought about it later he felt it was a bit daft, but soon felt an inward rebuke as they were used by God to bring reconciliation to the two warring factors in Siena, preventing bloodshed by their simplicity, innocence and love. Humility, simplicity, love and joy were the hallmarks of early Franciscan life, and it is significant that these virtues accompanied poverty of body and spirit.

The Mystery of God

By emphasising the primacy of joy over sorrow and misery,

I am not burying my head in the sand. I am well aware of the misery, poverty, violence and despair of our contemporary world, in our own country, and among many millions in a world which has gone astray. But unless we affirm the primacy of joy and hope we shall lose the war before we begin the battle! I meet social workers, community health workers and representatives from relief organisations who suffer from what I would call 'compassion fatigue'. They lose the battle out of discouragement. The discouragement sometimes comes from bureaucratic red tape, local opposition, political mismanagement, professional jealousy or government neglect, and threatens to reduce them to near-despair. The basic problem is that they are unable to affirm, or are unsure of, the primacy of joy and hope. If they could be undergirded and sustained by such a felt reality, then they could carry on in spite of opposition, discouragement and bungling.

I have just concluded a Quiet Day conducted for a local parish group, and among the participants was a professional woman who gives help and counsel to women who have just been diagnosed as having breast cancer, and other forms of the disease, and are awaiting surgery. The counselling continues also after the surgery. It is necessary for her not only to be positive and comforting to the patients under her care at a stressful time in their lives, but to be able to affirm the primacy of joy and hope in human life. She does not necessarily or ordinarily introduce the religious dimension into her professional life, which in any case would be most unwise in many cases – it is sufficient to be the channel of hope and healing for the patient whatever her condition.

Such affirmation of joy and hope was woven into the pattern of the spiritual life of the early Church when it suffered under pagan persecution – as it is part of the faith of the persecuted Church in many countries today. This perspective of joy and hope springs up in living Christian experience because its source is within the heart of God.

But let me share my pain as well as my joy in this respect. It would not be true or honest of me to maintain that things are quite as simple as I have made out. And without withdrawing any of the affirmative and positive statements I have made about the primacy of joy and hope, I would say that there have been and are times when I am perplexed and saddened about our world and the lack of clear and unequivocal evidence that joy and hope are basic to its structure.

This is the area in which I have to qualify some of the claims I have made above in the name of honesty, compassion and solidarity with those who suffer. There are times when I am faced with massive suffering, intolerable tensions, total inhumanity in the form of violence, torture, totalitarian regimes, and, in our century, forms of genocide. I sometimes cannot believe that we continue the proliferation of nuclear weapons and the sale of arms and military equipment to irresponsible and repressive regimes around the world.

I am alarmed and puzzled not only by man's inhumanity to man, not only by the cruelty we inflict on one another, but by the dreadful things that overtake us often without rhyme or reason like the increasing devastation caused by the Aids scourge. And close upon these are all the 'natural' disasters which manifest themselves in earthquakes, droughts, floods and ecological imbalance. Of course some of this can be explained, diagnosed, treated and cured – but most of it heaps up evidence which seems, to an impartial observer, to deny the primacy of joy and hope, and any affirmation of the divine Love.

But if I speak of an impartial observer, I am reminded of *both* pieces of evidence – that which speaks of joy, compassion, creativity, design, balance and harmony, and that which indicates alienation, misery, suffering, imbalance and destruction.

I hitched a lift with a van driver one day near Bournemouth. Seeing my brown habit, he was full of curiosity, and quickly informed me that he was an atheist. 'Well,' I said, 'I can't altogether blame you living in a world like this, but let me make a suggestion. You tell me why you are an atheist, and I'll tell you why I am a Christian.'

'It seems pretty obvious to me,' he replied. 'I'm faced with suffering, cruelty and inequality in the world and I can't believe in a God of love with all that around me.' He went on to illustrate his comments by the story of some children he had known who had been caught up in the disaster of a house fire.

'Ah yes,' I said, 'what you have been stating is what is called the problem of *evil* – which seems incompatible with a loving and caring God. But there is another problem, which is the problem of *good*, and it includes the rest of the evidence.'

'What do you mean?' he asked.

'Well, I see it like this,' I replied. 'For every bit of evidence you present which illustrates the evil, suffering, inequality and imbalance of the world, I can show you the opposite. I can point to harmony and beauty in the world, the regularity and productivity of the seasons, pattern and design in so much of the created order, sympathy and understanding among men and nations, laughter and singing of children's voices, and the self-sacrifice and compassion following every catastrophe that befalls any nation.' I continued in this vein, and we talked and shared in such a way that we both got caught up in our animated and lively discussion.

Suddenly, he said to me: 'What would you call a man who wasn't a Christian, but couldn't honestly be an atheist either?'

'There are a number of intermediate positions,' I replied, 'but I suppose you could call such a man an agnostic.'

'I suppose that just about describes me then,' he said with a wry smile. Neither of us had won an argument – but that's not what it was about. We both felt the pain of the situation and the weight of the evidence pointing both ways.

'Look', I said to him, 'in one sense I could say that it was a gamble, – "you pays your money and you takes your choice" – and I gamble myself on God . . .' He grinned at that, and the conversation went on. I spoke to him of 'other evidence' which I held in company with believers down the centuries, and I told him of my experience of the love of God in Jesus – but of course I was not marshalling evidence which he could weigh, measure and consider objectively – it carried us into the area of the mystery of human love and of divine love, and of God's identification with human suffering.

Such identification of God with human suffering is not the theme of this chapter, but I do want to say something about the mystery of God at this point. The first three chapters have tried to indicate the basic goodness and balance of the created order, its 'fall' and redemption. This chapter is by way of affirmation of the primacy of joy and hope, but we have hit up against contrary evidence in the state of our world. In the face of that there are at least two things to be said.

The first is that God himself not only comes to us in our misery and need, but that he takes upon himself the whole burden of our sin, sickness and death, and in the redemptive work of suffering, brings about a salvation and reconciliation which is in process of being worked out. The evidence for this is to be found in the living, suffering and redemptive experience of the people of God down through the ages, illustrated in the Old and New Testaments, among God's ancient people the Jews down to the present day, and within the fellowship of the Church. It is what the incarnation of God in Jesus is all about, including his suffering and death upon the cross and his resurrection from the dead. There is abundant testimony to all this, but it is a matter of faith-acceptance, and only those believe who will. That doesn't sound very satisfactory to a non-believer – and what I do at that point in conversation with such honest non-believers is to look at the human pattern of suffering, hope and love where it meets them in personal experience and in the world. There is much about that in other parts of this book.

But the second thing to be said concerns the mystery of God. Although I have weighty evidence from the great tradition and experience of the people of God down the ages, and although I have my own evangelical and gospel experience of the amazing forgiving love and overflowing joy of God in my own life – I am still faced with mystery. It is quite clear to me that God's ways are revealed *and* hidden. I both know him and do not know him. I both rejoice in him and weep with and for him. And I feel that I have only touched the edges of his ways, the hem of his garment. He does not behave in the way I would expect or desire, and 'if I were him' I can think of many ways in which I would act to justify my ways to men and to hurry along the work of redemption!

I cannot command God to appear, I cannot demand his love, I cannot make him justify his ways or persuade him to clarify his dealings. Faith and prayer are not magic, and God does not respond mechanically or answer automatically. There are times when he will answer neither my agonised weeping nor my seemingly profound faith. And what can I say about the mystery of love? Sometimes I weep in his absence because I need him so, or because my love for him calls out for his beauty to appear – but he does not come. And then when I least expect it, he touches me, sets me aflame, burns his own loveliness into my heart and takes me to himself in sheer glory and ecstasy.

The fact is that knowing so much, I know so little – and the more I get to know, the more I am faced with the dazzling darkness of the mystery and my own abysmal ignorance. But what I do know, what I have experienced, what I can feel and intuit only deepens my love, my faith, my trust. The outcome of my occasional anger, doubts, complainings and irreverence has been an eventual deepening of my faith. Out of some medical and pastoral experience and trying to avoid superficiality, I speak as a human being. From that perspective I have been faced with patience in the face of suffering, gentleness in the face of violence, joy in the midst of sorrow and victorious trust in the face of death.

The God I have learned to trust and love does not reveal to

me all his secrets. I only experience the manifestation of his love, his healing, his discipline and judgement. I have not gazed into the unutterable abyss of his being, and in writing these words I recall God's words to Moses when he asked to be shown God's glory; 'You cannot see my face; for man shall not see me and live.' And also the words of St Paul:

> . . . the blessed and only Sovereign, the King of kings and Lord of lords, who alone has immortality and dwells in unapproachable light, whom no man has ever seen or can see.[6]

In the Eastern churches a distinction is maintained between the 'essence' and the 'energies' of God. This means that God truly makes himself known in creation and redemption through his outflowing energies which are manifestations of his true nature – but humankind is not capable of gazing into the divine abyss of the essence of his being – for it is the abyss of mystery.[7]

The revelation of God in nature and in redemption is a true and saving expression of his being, and the mediatorship of Christ and the indwelling of the Holy Spirit are given to draw us ever deeper into the mystery of the Father. Jesus prayed in his high priestly prayer that we all may be drawn into such a participation in the divine trinitarian life that we may be united with the Father in his eternal glory even as Jesus himself was, before the foundation of the world. This is part of that ongoing process of redemption, and I believe that in eternity the revelation of that mystery will impart to us such knowledge and experience of the divine life that we shall be utterly confounded when faced with such unfathomable love. St Paul puts it like this: 'I consider that the sufferings of this present time are not worth comparing with the glory that is to be revealed to us.' And in a passage of power and beauty:

> O the depth and the riches and wisdom and knowledge of God! How unsearchable are his judgments and how inscrutable his ways! 'For who has known the mind of the Lord, or who has been his counsellor? Or who has given a gift to him that he might be repaid?' For from him and through him and to him are all things. To him be glory for ever. Amen.[8]

And I feel the reverberations of such glory in the lines of Faber:

> My God, how wonderful thou art,
> Thy majesty how bright,
> How beautiful thy mercy-seat
> In depths of burning light!
>
> O, how I fear thee, living God
> With deepest, tenderest fears,
> And worship thee with trembling hope,
> And penitential tears!

Trinitarian experience of joy

The shape of my experience of joy is triune! I mean that although my childhood had a great deal of solitude with some loneliness, and a great deal of sensitivity to the melancholy dimensions of creation and human suffering, yet there was a continual upsurge of joy. It seemed to me then, and it seems to me now, that the whole of nature is involved in a beautiful and harmonious game, a cosmic dance which moves in rhythmic joy in earth and sea and sky. Though there is an abyss of mystery concerning the incomprehensibility of the nature of God, yet the source and mainspring of joy within the divine essence bubbles up within the depths of my own soul. I cannot plumb my own depths, let alone the depths of God, but there in my own mystery I find an echo of the divine depths, and there is joy![9]

There have been times in my childhood – and they continue to this day – when the joy of creation has inebriated me – when I cannot help but dance and sing on the springy green turf, roll over in the surfing waves, jog alone along the seashore or sit reflectively with eyes and heart upon the setting sun. The joy of creation sometimes fills me with energy and enthusiasm and sometimes quietens me to contemplative stillness, but always lifts my mind and heart to the mystery of God.

So it is with the Gospel of Christ. I know what the New Testament documents are getting at when they speak of the unutterable joy of knowing and loving Jesus. The testimony of the early Church belongs to me and I greet the Lord Jesus with amazement and recognition:

> Jesus Christ . . . Without having seen him you love him; though you do not now see him you believe in him and rejoice with unutterable and exalted joy.[10]

I remember learning that whole chapter of the first epistle of Peter in the King James Version, and being bowled over by the wonder of it, especially in its rendering of the words 'joy unspeakable and full of glory'. How beautifully Charles Wesley experiences and communicates such joy:

> My God, I am thine,
> What a comfort divine,
> What a blessing to know that my Jesus is mine!
>
> In the heavenly Lamb
> Thrice happy I am,
> And my heart it doth dance at the sound of his name!
>
> True pleasures abound
> In the rapturous sound;
> And whoever hath found it hath paradise found.

My Jesus to know
And feel his blood flow,
'Tis life everlasting, 'tis heaven below.

Yet onward I haste
To the heavenly feast:
That, that is the fulness; but this is the taste!

And this I shall prove,
Till with joy I remove
To the heaven of heavens in Jesus's love.

If the Lord Jesus could endure the cross and shame of Calvary with joy,[11] then that same joy accompanies me on my pilgrimage with him through the pages of the New Testament and in the pattern of my earthly life. I am filled with wonder as I contemplate the story of his incarnation. I gaze with wonder as the Almighty stoops to the manger;

My God, contracted to a span,
Incomprehensibly made man!

I follow his childhood, his baptism, his temptation, his healing and saving ministry. I prostrate myself on the holy mount and feel the life-giving rays of his transfiguration, and weep with compassion as he sweats the blood-drops in Gethsemane. I follow the stations of the cross as he stumbles along the *Via Dolorosa*, bearing the burden of our sins to Calvary. And I am sore amazed as they crucify his sacred body and his blood comes streaming down the sky. Calvary!—the sad and mournful place where life and death contend, and the victory remains with love. Calvary!—the place where my sadness is turned to joy, where my darkness is turned to light, and where all the pain and grief of my life are shot through with the glory of the Easter morn.

It is joy, joy all the way—and this joy both redeems and

validates my sadness, for unless the pain and suffering are truly felt, then the joy of redemption cannot be truly experienced. There is no other way to glory save through the cross, for the thorns in the crown of Jesus also pierced his heart.

I am speaking of the trinitarian experience of joy, so the dimension of the Holy Spirit follows hard upon the heels of Jesus-joy. The risen Christ promised the gift of the Holy Spirit to the pentecostal Church, and on the day of Pentecost the promise was fulfilled in the outpouring of power, love and joy. Such was the effect of the mighty rushing wind and tongues of flame symbolising the Spirit's power, that the disciples were full of rejoicing and proclamation. Such was their spiritual inebriation that the onlookers and critics thought they were full of sweet wine.

Wherever the Holy Spirit was in evidence there was power, liberty, love and joy. Spiritual joy is not only one of the pentecostal gifts, but is also a fruit of the Spirit's indwelling. 'The kingdom of God is not food and drink,' says the apostle Paul, 'but righteousness and peace and joy in the Holy Spirit.' And writing to the Roman Christians he says: 'May the God of hope fill you with all joy and peace in believing, so that by the power of the Holy Spirit you may abound . . .'[12]

The charismatic gifts in the early church were manifestations of this pentecostal Spirit, and wherever the gifts abounded, there joy abounded too. In tongues and prophecy, in healing and discernment, in all the graces of the Spirit's manifestations there was joy and gladness of heart. These are the gifts which continue in Christ's Church today, and wherever there are loving, Spirit-filled Christians, they communicate infectious joy, contagious enthusiasm and radiant gladness of heart.

Well I remember as a lad of sixteen years of age, receiving an overwhelming baptism in the Holy Spirit. I was one of a small prayer group meeting in an upper room in Swansea to wait upon God for a deeper experience in the Holy Spirit.

Just as the meeting was about to close, I heard the police station clock strike ten – and I was thrown to the floor from a kneeling posture, and began to praise and adore God in a language I had never learned. I remember living through the next two hours in a state of joy and inebriation which I have since reckoned was akin to the apostles' experience on the day of Pentecost. Though a teetotaller I was drunk with joy and the Holy Spirit. The words in Acts 2:13 may be rendered 'sweet wine', and sweet it was, for I could not stand upon my legs, and I found it difficult to walk the two miles or so up Mount Pleasant hill to my home. I noted in my diary later that the inebriation lasted for six weeks, and then I was gently lowered into a semblance of normality.

In this chapter I have maintained that the source of true joy is the Holy Trinity, and the shape of my experience of joy is trinitarian. When I hear priests and pastors groan about the difficulties of preaching on Trinity Sunday I must say that I wonder about their trinitarian experience. Of course, the doctrine of the Holy Trinity is ineffable, incomprehensible and almost incommunicable without falling into emotionalism on the one hand and arid scholasticism on the other. The great Augustine said that it is almost impossible to speak of the Holy Trinity without falling into heresy! But if the experience of the early Church is the pattern of our life and ministry, then trinitarian joy should be the shape of our experience, and the joy should be communicable, infectious, enthusiastic – bringing gladness of heart to the Church and to the world.

I have also maintained that if we are able to affirm joy as an objective reality at the source of the natural world, and as the birthright of our human lives, then we shall be able to lift up the fallen and cheer the despondent with living faith and hope. Such an affirmation was the earliest preaching of the Gospel in the ministry of St Peter immediately after Pentecost when he declared:

> God anointed Jesus of Nazareth with the Holy Spirit and with power . . . He went about doing good and healing all that were oppressed by the devil, for God was with him.[13]

The triune Love is the source of all joy, and that joy is the inheritance of our humanity.

Notes

1 2 Peter 1:4
2 Job 38:7; Luke 15:7, 10.
3 Isaiah 12:3; Nehemiah 8:10; John 15:11; Romans 14:17; 1 Thessalonians 1:6.
4 Psalm 30:5; 126:5, 6.
5 Numbers 11:29.
6 Exodus 33:20; 1 Timothy 6:15, 16.
7 See Vladimir Lossky, 'Uncreated Energies', *The Mystical Theology of The Eastern Church* (London: James Clarke) pp. 67–90.
8 Romans 8:18; 11:33–36.
9 1 Corinthians 2:9–16.
10 1 Peter 1:8.
11 Hebrews 12:2.
12 Romans 14:7; 15:13.
13 Acts 10:38.

PART II:

The Context of Joy

5 Joy: Inheritance of Our Humanity

Joy, a basic ingredient

It is a difficult thing to define 'human nature' as if there were such a thing which is a given entity, capable of objective description. We *make* our human nature, it is a process, and we are all *in via*, on the way, participating in the human journey. But in trying to understand what is meant by the common humanity of which we are a part, there are certain basic ingredients which are part of any workable definition. For instance, I would affirm love as the most basic factor – and it is difficult enough to define love. But whatever we say about the primacy of love, joy is also a basic ingredient of our human experience.

'I tried to study philosophy,' the saying goes, 'but cheerfulness kept breaking in.' That's a grossly unfair caricature of philosophy, but we know what is meant. Cheerfulness is basic, it belongs to the very stuff of our human life, for joy and humour are human attributes which are indispensable to a well-rounded experience, and without which we cannot relate either to the world of nature or to our fellow human beings.

Of course that joy may manifest itself in various ways because we are all so diverse in temperament, background, racial inheritance and cultural traditions. There may be an upsurge, a flooding of our being, a bursting of the banks of our emotional and affective lives. Or it may reveal itself in a quiet bubbling spring of well-being. If joy and humour are absent from our common life of being and relationship in the world, then it is a serious matter. Melancholic depression reveals a basic defect in our make-up, and though there may arise problems and situations which afflict us in this way temporarily, if the condition becomes chronic then there is something terribly wrong.

On the other hand, though misery and sorrow are not basic to our humanity, they are nevertheless universal, and we are often invaded by such negative experiences. If, on the whole, we are psychically balanced, integrated and healthy, then we shall be able to cope with the problems. I am speaking of aspects of our mortality such as sickness, bereavement and the many disappointments and pains that frequently assail us. In fact, it is against such a background of mortal finitude that joy reveals itself in moments of unexpected help, comfort and strength which either well up from within, or are a gift of our corporate compassion for one another.

In the case of bereavement it is natural to grieve, to weep, to feel genuine sorrow and pain at the loss of a loved one. If that person was close and intimate then the process of grief may well take from eighteen months to two years to complete its course, and that is natural and good. But alongside that process of grieving there is a healing source within us which is natural to our humanity. This source will enable us to repattern our life so that out of the process of grief for the loved one there will emerge the reshaping of vocation and compassion for others that is akin to joy. The fact is that joy appears in greater clarity when we have known darkness and pain, for joy is the overcoming of negative forces in our lives. 'In the world you shall have tribulation,' says Jesus, 'but be of good cheer, I have overcome the world.'[1]

The fruit of the Spirit

The *fruit* of the Spirit is contrasted, in the New Testament, with the *works* of the flesh.[2] And joy is not worked up, strained after, sweated for. It is not something which is bought, borrowed or stolen. It is not specifically mentioned among the *gifts* of the Spirit,[3] but is among the fruit. A gift may be hung on a Christmas tree, but fruit can only grow!

Joy is inherent in our human life, and is meant to be manifested in every human being, but especially in the life of the believing Christian who is indwelt by the Holy Spirit of God. If the Spirit is indwelling and at work, then love, joy and peace should be in evidence in some measure. If the believer is living in the Holy Spirit then joy will flow, and others will catch the glow and be aware of the fragrance. The mixing of analogies here, namely the river of joy, the jewel of joy and the perfume of joy, all imply sharing – an overflow of joy from one to the other so that the personal experience becomes a corporate manifestation. *The Principles* of the First Order of the Society of St Francis lists joy among the three notes of the Order, and says:

> The brothers and sisters, rejoicing in the Lord always, must show forth in their lives the grace and beauty of divine joy. They must remember that they follow the Son of Man, who came eating and drinking, who loved the birds and the flowers, who blessed little children, who was the friend of publicans and sinners, who sat at the tables alike of the rich and the poor . . . They will mingle freely with all kinds of people, seeking to banish sorrow and to bring good cheer into other lives. They will carry with them an inner secret of happiness and peace which all will feel, if they may not know its source.[4]

This is not an encyclical of command, but a simple statement of the Franciscan way, exemplifying the humility, love and joy of the Gospel. *If* there is the love of God, union with Christ, and the indwelling of the Spirit, then joy will flow – nothing can stop it! Indeed, people expect to find joy in the heart and upon the face of the friar – and it must not be simulated.

I was hitching down the M5 some months back, from Worcester to Exeter, and I had a lift from a lorry-driver, and we both went into a transport café for a cup of tea. He was a macho, burly, good-humoured fellow, and soon a coach-load of schoolchildren came in. One of the lads looked over at me in my brown habit and called out: 'Are you Friar Tuck?'

'No,' I answered, grinning, 'but it's the same family!'

Looking at the driver, the boy then said: 'Who is he – Maid Marian?'

The driver shouted with laughter and shook his fist. The teacher then broke in: 'That's enough Williams', (or whatever the lad's name was). That's it! They *expected* humour, chaffing, teasing – JOY! And they got it!

In days of darkness

I have said that darkness, pain, sorrow is not basic to our humanity, but is invasive, parasitical, and yet it is always potentially present, and in a world like this it faces us on every side. The point about affirming that joy is basic is that it should be able to survive darkness, and it is always so encouraging to find people who have to face so much darkness and trouble in their lives and yet are able to draw upon the deep sources of joy and hope within themselves. *The Principles* go on to say:

> This joy, likewise, is a divine gift, and comes only from union with God in Christ. As such it can abide, even in days of darkness and difficulty, giving cheerful courage in the face of disappointment, and an inward serenity and confidence in sickness and suffering. Those who possess it can be content, for Christ's sake, with weakness, contempt, persecution, hardship and frustration; for when they are weak, then they are strong.[5]

We shall go on in the next chapter to indicate how we can mature through suffering and even manifest joy in the darkest days, but here let me say that the quality of joy which can surmount the darkest experiences of our lives has a supernatural quality about it. Joy is natural to our humanity, but in our poor, fallen, suffering world it is insufficient. It is often overwhelmed by the kinds of darkness that surround us in these days, and by the threatening clouds of doubt, depression and conflict which bombard us every day, at personal and corporate levels. But ancient words are a real promise and experience to those whose roots go deeper down than nature, deeper in God: 'Even though I walk through the valley of the shadow of death, I fear no evil; for thou art with me . . .' Commenting on this divine source of joy, *The Principles* are clear;

> These three notes of humility, love and joy, which should mark the lives of the brothers and sisters are all supernatural graces which can be won only from the divine bounty. They can never be attained through our own unaided exertions. They are miraculous gifts of the Holy Spirit. But it is the purpose of Christ our Master to work miracles through his servants; and if they will but be emptied of self and utterly surrendered to him, they will become chosen vessels of his Spirit and effective instruments of his mighty working, who is able to do immeasurably more than all we can ask or conceive.[6]

I said earlier that joy is not only a gift, but a fruit – something that is natural to the growth of the tree. In St John's teaching on Christ as the Vine and believers as the branches, fruit-bearing is part of the analogy. The teaching is simple and clear, and if only it were realised (literally real-ised) in the experience of the believer we should not be labouring under tomes of moral theology or struggling with ethical imperatives:

> Abide in me, and I in you. As the branch cannot bear fruit by itself, unless it abides in the vine, neither can you, unless you abide in me. I am the vine, you are the branches. He who abides in me, and I in him, he it is that bears the fruit, for apart from me you can do nothing.[7]

If we translate the theological and mystical truth of that passage into our daily lives, then the mainspring and motive of our existence will be the hidden, interior life of Christ, and the indwelling Spirit which is the rising sap of the vine will manifest itself in the fruitbearing of love, joy, peace – and the rest . . .

Jesus goes on in this chapter to instruct his disciples in the qualities of love and joy. He assures them of the Father's love, and of the importance of abiding in that love which leads to fruit-bearing, and then he says: 'These things have I spoken to you, that my joy may be in you, and that your joy may be full.'

The universal Spirit

When I think of joy as the inheritance of our humanity I am aware of thinking not solely in Christian terms. There is a universal experience of God which is preparatory to the Jesus of history, but which is, nevertheless, an experience of the Eternal Word. There is a lovely and diverse richness in trinitarian faith. It means that the divine Presence is universal and excludes no-one who seeks for God in love, honesty and truth. God the Father is the tremendous mystery that lies within and behind all things, unknowable in his divine essence, who creates and redeems by the Eternal Word and the Holy Spirit. God the Son is the creative Word by whom the Father created all things and who indwells everyone who is born into the world.[8] The Holy Spirit is he who at the creation moved and brooded over the face of the great deep, and as the Lord and life-giver breathed the life of God into the whole created order.[9]

So the whole of creation is indwelt and inspired by the Holy Trinity, and as the Father, Son and Holy Spirit interpenetrate and mutually indwell one another in the mystery and unity of the Godhead, so our humanity is called to share in the creative and redemptive life of God.

The old theologians used to distinguish between common and special grace. Common grace includes the gracious acts and mercies of God which come to us as sunshine, rain and all the common blessings of our natural lives. Special grace indicates the revelatory acts of God in the Old and New Testaments in prophecy and redemption. The Christian Church, East and West, Catholic and Protestant, has at times exclusivised such mercies and denied them to all save those who specifically recognised the historical Jesus. The early Church and the Church in our day understands a little more clearly that God is continually at work in every part of the world, wherever there are those who are open to his Holy Spirit. This means that there is no man, woman or child who is completely forsaken by God, for the very air that we breathe is a physical manifestation of the divine *ruach Yahweh*, the breath of God. The image of God in man may be distorted, damaged and perverted beyond the aid of man to regenerate, but it is not completely destroyed. There are traces of God within the world and within our humanity.

I have said that joy is universal, and that is because the Spirit is universal. Christians cannot compromise the uniqueness of Christ or place him in a pantheon among other gods, but certainly the presence of the cosmic Christ, the universal Word can be recognised in all that is true and good and beautiful in every culture.

In the past the Church has been guilty of destroying human cultures, languages and traditions, and even, as Thomas Merton says, of taking the Gospel of Christ (or our version of it) with cannon and sword. It is right and good to seek to share the riches of Christ throughout the world, but how much better it would have been if we had carried the love of Christ to other peoples, intent at the same time on discovering the hidden Christ already dwelling in their cultures and traditions.

There were times when this did happen, of course. The story of Matthew Ricci and the early Jesuit missions in China are an example of this, when the title and garments of a mandarin were given to the missionary Jesuits because they had earned them, and because they actually shared in the wisdom traditions of the people to whom they had gone to share the Gospel of Christ.[10] At such times it was possible to share the joy of the historical Jesus, mingling it with the discovery of the etenal Word.

Thomas Merton, writing of the wisdom of ancient Taoism in the fourth century BC, reproduces the following meditation called *The Breath of Nature* which is a beautiful commentary on the presence of the Holy Spirit in creation as the breath of God:

> When great Nature sighs, we hear the winds
> Which, noiseless in themselves,
> Awaken voices from other beings,
> Blowing on them.
> From every opening
> Loud voices sound. Have you not heard
> This rush of tones?
>
> There stands the overhanging wood
> On the steep mountain:
> Old trees with holes and cracks
> Like snouts, maws, and ears,
> Like beam-sockets, like goblets,
> Grooves in the wood, hollows full of water:
> You hear mooing and roaring, whistling
> Shouts of command, grumblings,
> Deep drones, sad flutes.
> One call awakens another in dialogue.
> Gentle winds sing timidly,
> Strong ones blast on without restraint.
> Then the wind dies down. The openings
> Empty out their last sound.
> Have you not observed how all then trembles and subsides?

Yu replied: I understand:
The music of earth sings through a thousand holes.
The music of man is made on flutes and instruments.
What makes the music of heaven?

Master Ki said:
Something is blowing on a thousand different holes.
Some power stands behind all this
and makes the sounds die down.
What is this power?[11]

This is a devotional and experiential exposition of the Hebrew *ruach*, or the Greek *pneuma*, both of which words in the Old and New Testaments are used for breath, wind, spirit and Spirit. The same universal sense of presence is felt in Psalm 104;

> O Lord, how manifold are thy works!
> In wisdom hast thou made them all;
> the earth is full of thy creatures.
> These all look to thee,
> to give them their food in due season.
> When thou givest it to them, they gather it up;
> when thou openest thy hand,
> they are filled with good things
> When thou hidest thy face, they are dismayed;
> when thou takest away their breath, they die
> and return to their dust.
> When thou sendest forth thy Spirit, they are created;
> and thou renewest the face of the ground.

The Spirit as the wind and breath of God is well represented in Christian hymnology, and the mighty rushing wind of Pentecost is a clear manifestation of the Spirit's power, recalling the life-giving breath of God in the prophecy of Ezekiel.[12] Jesus speaks of the mystery of the wind of nature when he says to Nicodemus: 'The wind blows where it wills, and you hear the sound of it, but you do not know whence it comes or whither it goes; so is everyone who is born of the Spirit.'

In ancient Celtic spirituality the Trinity is often invoked in the context of earth and wind, sea and sky. St Patrick's Breastplate is a well-wrought poetic pattern of creation and redemption which should be read (and sung) in its entirety, but a few stanzas from C.P. Alexander's version will illustrate what I mean:

> I bind unto myself today
>   The strong name of the Trinity
> By invocation of the same,
>   The Three in One, and One in Three.
>
> I bind unto myself today
>   The virtues of the star-lit heaven,
> The glorious sun's life-giving ray,
>   The whiteness of the moon at even,
> The flashing of the lightning free,
>   The whirling wind's tempestuous shocks,
> The stable earth, the deep salt sea,
>   Around the old eternal rocks.
>
> I bind unto myself the name,
>   The strong name of the Trinity:
> By invocation of the same,
>   The Three in One, and One in Three.
> Of whom all nature hath creation;
>   Eternal Father, Spirit, Word;
> Praise to the Lord of my salvation,
>   Salvation is of Christ the Lord.[13]

Celtic spirituality is a useful illustration here of the universal nature of a trinitarian faith. St Patrick did not run from nature into grace (as if they could be separated) when he sought to proclaim the Gospel at the hill Tara in the fifth century. He lit a bonfire in defiance of the heathen king, to herald the resurrection of Jesus, and used natural symbols and analogies to portray the Gospel of Christ.

As I write these words I am in the chaplain's room at the top of the guesthouse of our enclosed sisters at Oxford, and the March winds are blowing, causing the trees over all the convent grounds to dance and tremble in the gale. Especially there are two giant trees in the distance, jubilant with joy, and dancing with ecstatic delight as the breath of God shakes them, causing them to quiver and bend. As I watch them now, they cause my imagination to run riot, inviting me to join them in their cosmic and universal dance of joy.

The Holy Spirit in the unconscious

Making an interior pilgrimage into the depths of one's own being is both a joyful and a fearful journey. There are depths within man's own being, as well as within the divine Being, which are beyond rational comprehension[14], and the use of depth psychology in the service of Christian faith is of great help as the great truths and symbols of scripture resound in the depths of our contemporary spiritual experience.

Let me illustrate by present experience – for there is something wrong unless the reality of God impinges upon the present moment, whether of light or darkness. I am fulfilling my chaplain's duty at the sisters' convent here at Freeland, near Oxford. A few days ago I had to see my spiritual director also in Oxford, and wondered how to put to her what was happening in the present part of my spiritual journey. The night before I saw her, being open to the Lord, I had a dream which contained the basic symbol and clear meaning of what we had to share and explore together – that's another story. But last night, I had a dream, and coupled with today's Old Testament reading at mass it communicates another clear message from the Holy Spirit at work in my unconscious.[15]

In my dream I entered the cloister of a church/monastery.

(A cloister is a communicating passage running around the inside of a monastic building.) I was familiar with this cloister and had trodden it previously, but on this occasion, as soon as I entered it I found myself on my tummy because the ceiling had descended toward the ground, leaving barely two feet between. Ordinarily, this would have caused symptoms of apprehension and fear, but on this occasion, without undue fear, I found the constriction merely uncomfortable, and was aware that I must get out of the situation. It seemed to me pointless to go forward because I had the awareness that if I did, the constriction would increase, and I would be trapped. Therefore, I did a turn-around, and slowly moved out of the threatening area of the cloister and crawled into the open air where there was a lifting of the threat, an ability to breathe freely and a sense of liberation and expansive freedom. I awoke, aware of the dream, and allowed it to bear its own interpretation into my conscious mind. This was a clear example to me of my unconscious mind making available its intuitive understanding and knowledge to my conscious mind, in a similar way to that in which Joseph of the Old Testament and Joseph of the New Testament, as well as many others, allowed God to speak to them through their dreams.[16]

It is not enough to dream, one must interpret. I shared last week's dream (all about a lion) with my spiritual director, and we talked of its interpretation together. But last night's dream contained its own interpretation. It had to do with the basic joy and creativity which is at the heart of our humanity – the theme of this chapter. I 'heard' through this dream the counsel of the Holy Spirit speaking through my unconscious mind, to the effect that I must not allow conventional or ecclesiastical religion (symbolised by the cloister) to cramp my style or to dictate the content of my theological understanding. If one lives for ecclesiastical religion and surrenders the life-giving insights of nature and grace to its organisation and demands, then one enters into a constricting situation which will eventually asphyxiate – strangle the life out of you!

Now I did not come to the conclusion in the small hours of this morning that I should move out of the religious life or the monastic tradition, for that has been life-giving for me. Nor did I think that as chaplain to an enclosed Order I should suddenly tell all the sisters at mass this morning to 'up and go' – though that is sometimes necessary for an individual who is not called or suited to the enclosed life of prayer.

But I listened to the dream and realised a number of things which were clearly confirmed by a beautiful reading of the Old Testament lesson by one of the sisters at mass this morning. The wonderful thing is that I have time this morning to write it up at this point in this chapter. God's gifts are well-timed!

The reading was from the forty-seventh chapter of Ezekiel – a favourite of mine, anyway, for Ezekiel was one of those ecstatic prophets who was open to the gentle and violent movement of the Holy Spirit through dream, vision, prophecy and prophetic symbolism. One only has to read his vision of the Valley of Dry Bones to feel the intensity and vibrancy of his prophetic and mystical vision. Chapter forty-seven describes with powerful symbolism the river of life which has its source springing up from the altar within the temple of God. The angelic being brought Ezekiel from its source in the temple, through various geographical locations to see that the life-giving river flowed into the wilderness, bringing life, sweetness and fruitfulness everywhere it went in the arid and desert wilderness. It sweetened all the salty and brackish waters wherever it came into contact with them, it was filled with a multiplicity of freshwater fish, and the trees and shrubs which sprang up on its banks bore foliage and fruit for the healing of the nations.[17]

The other important element in this story is that the prophet found that there were depths within depths in this divine river. He paddled in it, walked through it, waded in it, swam in it, and acknowledged that it was over his head and deeper than his depths. Carl Jung says that we have our ordinary, conscious mind which operates in our day-to-day relationships of association and learning. Beneath that, as it were, lies the huge area of our *personal unconscious* in which are hidden and stored information, abilities and intuitions which we know, but which the conscious mind cannot call up or command at will. Beneath that there is the *collective unconscious*, which is the dimension or realm of *archetypal symbols*, such as we have in my own dream and in the vision of Ezekiel. They are life-giving symbols of creative and destructive power, and the emphasis given by Jung is the healing and life-giving nature of these symbols. He also believes that we should be open and willing to listen to our personal and collective unconscious, for not only can we receive help and direction for our daily lives, but in psychical hurts and sickness, there is a natural healing power, akin to the physical healing power which resides in the body for the healing of wounds and fractures. In a theological sense we may say that God speaks to us in and through our collective (Ezekiel) and personal (my dream) unconscious, in prophetic and personal revelation and guidance.[18]

So we gathered at the altar this morning, sisters and guests in an encircling fellowship of prayer and love, listening to this Ezekiel reading, and I felt the joy of God flow through me, interpreting and fulfilling the dream of last night. It was clear to me that on the one hand there is a kind of religion and philosophy which is constricting, deadening, ecclesiastical. It has to do with the bureaucratic machinery and talking-shops of the organised Church. And there is the life-giving joy, compassion and healing river of life which overflows and communicates the divine love in a world of need. It originates and springs up from the throne and altar of God – but it moves out and into the desert, carrying life and fertility wherever it goes, and its fruits are for healing and compassion. The throne and the altar within the temple indicate that it is the life of God – not just an humanitarian and free spirit which springs up unaided from our poor humanity. Nevertheless, it flows into and through our humanity.

In my ministry among Christians and non-Christians in the pulpit, at conferences, groups and retreats, and hitch-hiking on the road constantly in conversation with secular people, I find similar things being expressed. They concern the Church and the world. There is a recognition that there are saintly, joyful and compassionate people who are followers of Christ, but a general feeling about the Church, born of bitter experience, is of its lack of sensitivity, inability to feel heights of joy or depths of sorrow, and the irrelevance of its message.

I have no wish to be simplistic or to caricature the Church, for I am part of it, and an ordained priest and friar within it. But I am continually saddened about its deadness and impotence on the one hand, and its aggressive arrogance and inflexibility on the other. And so often those who endeavour to avoid the establishment respectability with its deadness, and its Evangelical or Catholic arrogance, find themselves frenetically involved in charitable organisations. Because of a lack of interior tranquillity they are anxiously active, unable to rest, and often not in touch with their deeper selves.

Now this sounds somewhat judgmental, and of course there is an element of judgment in it, for with discernment comes judgment born of both truth and compassion. My dream of last night and the reading from Ezekiel indicate both the negative diagnosis and the positive prescription which I must take to heart, and which I am concerned to communicate here. It is that when we are constricted (the cloister dream) by a narrow and prejudiced religious view and practice, or by a manner of life which is lacking in openness, dialogue and the freedom to breathe freely in our world, then a 'turning about' or conversion becomes necessary. Such openness, dialogue and freedom indicate that God is the source of our joy and compassion (as in the Ezekiel vision). It is not God that is proscribed, but pseudo-religion. Bad religion promotes prejudice, violence, holy war, negative condemnation and alliance with worldy powers which compromise the Gospel.

Living faith is seeing the joy and goodness of God in every situation. Starting from where we are, we can then allow such joy and goodness to overflow our own lives, communicating itself to other human beings in positive relationships, and to the natural order in compassion–like Ezekiel's river. The latter involves not only a contemplative perspective of the world but also an ecological awareness.

The vision of Ezekiel was a corrective to my dream as well as an exposition of it. I needed to see that legalistic and organisational preoccupation with religion was narrow, constrictive and suffocating. But that does not mean that there is no place for church, scripture and sacraments. The opposite is true. But it is necessary to see that Church must be in the way of love. If it is not experiencing and communicating the love and mystery of God in prayer, compassion and life-giving faith, it is being unfaithful to the Lord. Bad religion is far worse than no religion, for there are many humanists who follow the hiddenness of the Holy Spirit in their concern and compassion for the helpless and needy of our world. And there are many non-Christians who are relentless in their honest search for truth, and have rejected what they think is the faith of Christ because of the example set by a worldly and unspiritual Church.

To get back to the dream and the vision. It was one example of how the Holy Spirit within my own unconscious, and within the prophetic interior life of Ezekiel, spoke a word in synchronicity today. Carl Jung uses the term *synchronicity* to indicate that there is a certain appropriate timing of incidents in our lives which indicates that something is going on at a deeper level, bringing together creative moments which confirm our interior life and search. He was not writing of the Christian doctrine of providence, but the application is appropriate. I am concerned to point out that such creative sources lie at the heart of our humanity. The way I put it earlier was that joy is a basic ingredient of our humanity, and that it is an indication that there is meaning at the heart of our existence. We are not washed up as flotsam and jetsam on the beach of secular existence, but are caught up in the larger designs of a loving creator and redeemer. Though much of this is not superficially obvious, yet for those who wait upon God, who search in the depths of their own hearts and are open and lovingly patient to their own unconscious depths, it will yield its treasures.

We are made for joy, and we are called to join in the universal joy for which we were made. Everything on earth that brings us joy can lead us to God. But if we endeavour to make joyful things ends in themselves, then we shall suffer the pain of restless longing and fall short of finding our ultimate joy in God the source of all.

We must not deny, barter or fritter away our inheritance, but recognise it, claim it and live it, for joy is the inheritance of our common humanity, and participation in it awaits you and me today!

Notes

1 John 16:33 (AV).
2 Galatians 5:16–25
3 1 Corinthians 12:1–11.
4 *The Principles*, 28.
5 Ibid., 29.
6 Ibid., 30.
7 John 15:4, 5.
8 See the Prologue to John's Gospel, 1:1–18.
9 Genesis 1:1, 2; 2:7.
10 See 'The Jesuits in China'. Thomas Merton, *Mystics and Zen Masters* (New York: Dell Publishing Co.) pp. 81–90.
11 Thomas Merton, *The Way of Chuang Tzu* (London: Unwin Books) pp. 38f.
12 Acts 2:1, 2; Ezekiel 37:1–10

13 *The English Hymnal* No. 212, vv. 1, 4, 9.
14 1 Corinthians 2:11.
15 For an exposition of the work of Carl Jung in Christian perspective, see Christopher Bryant, *Depth Psychology and Religious Belief*, *The River Within*, *The Heart in Pilgrimage* and *Jung and the Christian Way*, all published by Darton, Longman and Todd.
16 Genesis 37:5–11; Matthew 1:18–25.
17 There is a relation between Ezekiel's vision and that of St John the Divine depicted in the new Paradise of God. See Ezekiel 47:1–12; Revelation 22:1–7.
18 See especially Christopher Bryant, *Jung and the Christian Way*.

6 Maturing Through Suffering

The burden of suffering

There is a kind of writing and preaching that almost makes light of suffering, either to indicate that this world is a vale of tears and discipline, or to highlight the glory that is to come. Such a superficial understanding of suffering reveals only that the writer or preacher has not descended into the depths of physical, mental or spiritual affliction.

As I write these words I call to mind some of the requests for prayer that we are holding before God in our monastery at the present time: a lad of seven years dying of leukemia; a girl of fifteen in a coma, suffering from encephalitis; a young man of twenty-four with inoperable cancer. And I am aware of my own sorrow which involves my father's frail condition. As well as his increasing deterioration through emphysema, he contracted a double cataract which suddenly plunged him into total blindness in spite of surgery which was unsuccessful. He is at present in hospital, moving simply from bed to chair and back again in great vulnerability, and I sit with him frequently, holding his hand, sharing in prayer his tears and sadness.

Far be it from me, then, to speak of the nobility of suffering – it can often be destructive, indiscriminate and soul-destroying. To invoke 'the will of God' over suffering of the kind referred to above is to come near to a kind of blasphemy, and only those who have known such suffering have the right to pronounce judgment or make an evaluation of its meaning or merits.

Having said that, I am constantly amazed at the way in which the victims of suffering find that there is a depth of trust, love and hope beneath the layers of sorrow and pain they experience. A priest who has been a constant retreatant here at Glasshampton over the last decade or so contracted motor neurone disease some two or three years back, and his physical condition rapidly deteriorated reducing his mobility and co-ordination. Finally he was taken into a nursing home to die. The last time he came on retreat, one of our older friars said to me: 'The worse Andrew's condition gets, the saintlier he becomes.' His sister spoke to me last week and told me that the last month in the nursing home he radiated such peace and acceptance that those who nursed him became aware of an inner sustaining strength that remained with him right to the end. One has only to read of the work, experience and attitude of people like Dame Cicely Saunders and the Hospice movement, and Dr Elizabeth Kübler-Ross, to learn how, in experience, many people in terminal illness manifest not only hope, but joy and humour, and face death with an equilibrium that reveals an immense hidden vitality within our common humanity.

But such discoveries of hope and optimism do not detract from the burden of pain and suffering that many people have to carry themselves, or on behalf of suffering relatives and loved ones. There is a burden to be borne, and sometimes it persists over a period of years, and demands physical and emotional energy that can be exhausting. Some people go on for years ignoring this dimension of suffering burying their heads in the sand of hedonism – then when it strikes their family or their own lives, they react in bitterness. Others use the false props of pseudo-religion, or wrongly appropriate the values of true religion, keeping their heads in the clouds of other-worldliness. Such euphoric clouds clear away when the icy winds of ravaging sickness, crippling disease or sudden bereavement blow with a disillusioning vengeance.

Variations in attitude

Those who work in medical, nursing and caring professions,

or in any capacity of compassionate concern for the sick and disabled, soon find that it is not so much the seriousness or incapacitating power of the disease, but the attitude of the sufferer that makes life positive or negative. It is sheer joy to visit or care for some people who have little going for them in terms of physical or mental ability, for their attitude to life depends upon an interior source of joy. With various degrees of disability, they actually 'enjoy' life.

But there are others who suffer less, who are less disabled, who have no financial or domestic worries, who are self-pitying, constantly complaining, will make no effort for themselves, and who make other people's lives around them a misery. These attitudes become self-perpetuating, for the former patient will inspire joy and hope, encourage visitors, and will use whatever possibilities remain for tasks of body and mind which increase creativity. The lattter group will discourage visitors, increase surrounding gloom, make little or no attempt at creative tasks, and fulfil their own negative prophecies about the worthlessness of their own lives. The first group will mature through suffering, the second group will deteriorate. Such attitudes apply not only to physical and mental suffering, but also to the various experiences and challenges that face us during our lives, demanding change, courage and versatility. Let me illustrate what I mean.

In his book *When Bad Things Happen to Good People*, Rabbi Harold Kushner tells the story of his son, Aaron, and of the amazing maturity of experience that has been his through Aaron's disease and eventual death at fourteen years of age. The child, up to nearly two years of age, was bright and intelligent, but from eight months had stopped gaining weight, and his hair began to fall out, causing increased concern and worry, until at three years of age the paediatrician diagnosed 'progeria' or rapid aging. Aaron would never grow much beyond three feet in height, would have no hair on his head or body, would look like a little old man while he was still a child, and would die in his early teens – all of which happened. Kushner was a young rabbi, and he charts his feelings at the time. He had dedicated his life to God, and with his wife was serving a local Jewish congregation in Boston. Many people can identify with his feelings:

> . . . Even if I could persuade myself that I deserved this punishment for some sin of neglect or pride that I was not aware of, on what grounds did Aaron have to suffer? He was an innocent child, a happy, outgoing three-year old. Why should he have to suffer physical and psychological pain every day of his life? Why should he have to be stared at, pointed at, wherever he went? Why should he be condemned to grow into adolescence, see other boys and girls begin to date, and realise that he would never know marriage or fatherhood? It simply didn't make sense.[1]

At that time as a young rabbi, Kushner had grown up with an image of God as an omniscient, omnipotent father-figure who would treat us as earthly parents do – or better. He believed in God's discipline, but a fair justice that would protect from harm and see that we got what we deserved in life. There was, of course, the awareness of dark tragedy in the world – fatal accidents, crippling diseases, mental illness and sudden terminal diagnoses, but such things had not struck personally, there was the idea that God knew more about the world than he did and that it would all ultimately work out somehow. Then the tragedy encapsulated him in the diagnosis of Aaron's disease, as progeria struck a blow which shook Rabbi Kushner and his wife to their foundations.

The result of all this, joined with the years of suffering, nursing, prayerful crying, complaining and reflecting upon the tragedy, is spelled out in the book which is challengingly born out of real experience. He unfolds his experience out of his need to share both the pain and the emerging discoveries of faith. He writes also to help other people who find themselves in a similar predicament, or who want to go on believing but whose anger at God makes it hard for them to retain their faith, and for those whose devotion to God leads them to blame themselves for their suffering, persuading themselves that they deserve it.

Kushner's experience at the time was that there were not many books and not many people who could help him. The books he turned to were concerned with defending God's honour, with logical proof that bad is really good and that evil is necessary to make this a good world. They did not minister to the bewilderment and anguish of the father of a dying child. As he says: 'They had answers to all of their own questions, but no answer for mine.'

Aaron died two days after his fourteenth birthday, and the scripture passage which ministered to Rabbi Kushner during that period came out of the bitter experience of King David:

> When David saw the servants whispering, he said to them, Is the child dead? And they said, He is dead. And David rose and washed and changed his clothing and asked that food be set before him, and he ate. The servants said to him, What is this that you are doing? You fasted and wept for the child when he was alive, and now that he is dead, you get up and eat! And David said: While the child was yet alive, I fasted and wept, for I said, Who knows whether the Lord will be gracious to me, and the child will live! But now that he is dead, why should I fast? Can I bring him back again? I shall go to him; but he will not return to me.[2]

In writing of the experience he says that he went beyond self-pity to the point of facing and accepting Aaron's death, and had come to the place where he wanted not only to share the hurt of it all, but to bear witness to the source of strength and courage he experienced in God. One of the powerful things I felt in the reading of this book was the simple and transparent honesty which comes across through the pain – there is a joy which lies beneath the surface, and an attitude of integrity that pulls one up short. There is also a certain unorthodoxy about theology and experience that somehow deepens faith, and I could only sigh with compassionate understanding when he writes:

> I am a more sensitive person, a more effective pastor, a more sympathetic counsellor because of Aaron's life and death than I would ever have been without it. And I would give up all of those gains in a second if I could have my son back. If I could choose, I would forgo all the spiritual growth and depth which has come my way because of our experiences, and be what I was fifteen years ago, an average rabbi, an indifferent counsellor, helping some people and unable to help others, and the father of a bright, happy boy. But I cannot choose.[3]

'I cannot choose.' That is the point. We are faced with suffering which often does not have any obvious meaning. If there was a deep, interior meaning, the bearing of pain for another's good, a surrendering of faculties that another may have fulness of life, then the suffering could be borne, even with a certain joy. But we are faced personally, corporately, in our world, with senseless, meaningless and absurd suffering, cruelty, carnal wastage and bloodshed that bears no meaning – and we have no choice. But as Rabbi Kushner says, the question we should be asking is not: 'Why did this happen to me? What did I do to deserve this?' This is often an unanswerable and pointless question. Better to ask; 'Now that this has happened to me, what am I going to do about it?'

If we become bitter, cynical, disillusioned, then we may take the path which leads to depression, despair, and either hatred or suicide. Our suffering, if it is a fact of our existence and experience, can be turned to serve God or the devil. The image of a man living and dying in what used to be called a lunatic asylum seems only to call the goodness and love of God into question, but when such a man writes upon the wall of his cell the following words, what are we to say about the riches of his interior life?

> Could we with ink the ocean fill,
> Or were the sky of parchment made,
> Were every blade of grass a quill
> And every man a scribe by trade;
> To write the love of God above
> Would drain the ocean dry;
> Nor could the scroll contain the whole
> Though stretched from sky to sky.

Maturity through suffering means that people who really suffer gain the victory. They impose meaning on meaningless situations because they have a rich, interior life of faith which has been burned and tested in the crucible of suffering, and has emerged the richer, the deeper, with more compassion and an understanding that generates not only sympathy but joy. It is not only that God suffers in and with those who suffer, but he also inspires men and women to self-sacrificing dedication in giving their lives for the alleviation of suffering and the promotion of hope, health, justice and joy. God does not, in some omnipotent manner, direct suffering, plagues, drought and disasters only to bad people, but bears the pain and tragedy of all who will look to him, inspiring interior hope and help for their healing. It is a strange thing, but once you set your face against evil and suffering, and ally your energies with life, light and love, then everything takes on a different face, a new value. I remember going into the infirmary in Worcester some years ago with a Baptist minister friend who was also a part-time male nurse in one of the medical wards. I went up to one of the screened beds where an eleven-year-old boy was dying with a brain tumour. My friend took his hand, gently held him close for he was very sore, and spoke quietly into his ear. Such was the communication of love between them that I was wonderfully shaken by the effect of joy and sorrow within me. I was perceiving not only the suffering of God in the dying child, but the compassion of God in a man who loved – both spiritually and physically as his pastor and nurse.

I realise with sadness that this is not very common. One has to be a person of compassion and contemplation to enter into such a relationship. On another occasion I took one of the members of my Cardiff congregation along to the psychiatric hospital where I was to celebrate the eucharist for the patients. I did not realise the effect this would have upon him, for it was his first visit. They came to the chapel in their usual way, stumbling, dribbling, chattering and talking to themselves. I greeted them, hugged them, 'played' with them – and it didn't matter if they didn't understand the words, talked through the readings, laughed through the hymns – the Lord understood. But it shook Antony – the very look and feel of such disorientation shocked and frightened him. It caused tears of charity and compassion – an altogether necessary experience which led to a deepening of maturity through suffering.

Maturity in facing situations

I could go on drawing on my own and others' experiences in facing of suffering and death with a certain joy and maturity. The 'serious and humorous' account of Richard Lamberton's medical care of terminally ill patients and their relatives in his *East End Doc* is enough to make the reader laugh and cry in the self-same paragraph.[4] But we are not always facing life-and-death situations. Our suffering may be found in our everyday lives in sudden confrontation with challenges, expectations, emotional frustrations and entanglements, and a hundred and one other things which beget and enforce attitudes in us for good or ill. We may be involved in a process of continuing openness, flexibility and maturity, or of prejudice, alienation and fixity, leading to frustration and deterioration.

One of the important areas in which we may experience

suffering, especially if we are somewhat introvert and sensitive in temperament, is childhood. Even now, with all the understanding communicated through the work of modern psychiatric practice and the general awareness of the importance of infant and childhood experiences and impressions, we fail to trace our pains and problems to these early roots. The first lesson in affirmation or rejection, in outgoing love or negative turning – in upon oneself may be experienced in childhood – both maturity and disintegration begin there! 'Each victory will help you some other to win' is not only true of temptation but of the positive facing and acceptance of childhood experiences and challenges as they occur.

It was at twelve years of age that I underwent a definite conversion experience – a personal turning to Christ as Saviour, Friend and Brother. At that time I was attending a sort of 'rough-neck' school which was very good for me because of my shyness, but also very scary and demanding because there was bullying at personal and group levels. The most feared of the school gangs was called 'the black spot gang', so-named because its sign was an indelible black spot imprinted on the wrist, just hidden by the sleeve. If you did not have such a spot you were 'done over', but if you forged such a spot to evade a beating you were 'doubly done over' for arrogance – a kind of Morton's fork!

Not belonging to the gang, I took refuge in a small, ineffectual gang, which indulged in a bit of smoking and swearing to prove our manhood and virility! I was averse to both these things anyway, but when I had the experience of conversion it was not only a change of heart and mind, but an infusion of moral strengths and stamina – a whole theology of conversion in my twelve-year-old experience. Anyway, I decided it was time to call a halt. So I quietly dissociated myself from the gang, risking the consequences both from them and the black spot terrors. Prayer didn't save me from the consequences I most feared (it rarely does), but did give me the strength to face it and get the victory over it.

One day, the gang members came asking why I was not joining in their occult activities, and on being told that I had become a Christian, they were not amused. So they huddled together to find a solution which would consist both of discipline and revenge. The next day we had woodwork lessons in a neighbouring school, and during the recreation time, I was surrounded by the eight or nine members of the gang in the school yard. 'Now, Lloyd,' they warned, 'we have decided that you must swear and join the gang again.'

'Well, I'm not going to,' I said – upon which a long hat-pin was produced which one of the boys had pinched from his mother's hat, and I was threatened.

'If you won't swear, we'll stick this into you,' and I needn't say which part of my anatomy it was directed towards.

Anyway, swear I would not, and stick they did. Eventually I was saved by the bell. The next day, back at our own school, the headmaster came into the class. 'Stand up, Lloyd,' he commanded. And I did so. 'Now,' he said, 'can you tell me anything that happened yesterday in the Hafod school yard!'

'No, sir,' I replied, meaning that I could not because I would not grass on the others.

'Alright,' he said, 'can anyone tell me about an incident that happened involving Lloyd – and some others?' Silence. Shuffling. Eyes down. Then: 'Up on your feet the following boys . . .' and he enumerated all the lads concerned. I don't know how he found out, but everyone knew that I had not told him. Anyway, there followed a precise, psychological, effectual interrogation that elicited a confession from one, then another – until the whole set-up became clear.

Corporal punishment was the regime at that school, and although I would not have agreed with it as a child, and feel myself 'agin it' now, there was a sort of rough-and-ready justice about it which was recognised by the lads generally. It appeared I was a kind of mini-hero, and I was a bit confused as to why this should be so. It appeared that not only had I suffered silently, but I was not prepared to grass on the others, cost what it may. Now this incident is quite clear in my mind decades later because it was a formative experience – an illustration of a maturity through suffering that stood me in good stead for the future challenges to faith and life that have come my way. The world of the child, perhaps especially of a young and sensitive boy, can be a very threatening world. My home and parental background was emotionally secure, and my religious experience was a tremendous source of strength – the combination of these two enabled me to stand *contra mundum*, against the world, because I was assured of the rightness of my stand.

Maturity, an evolving process

The experience of the last paragraphs, though I can chuckle about it now, was an experience of suffering in that I was a child, alone, losing my friends, standing for a cause which had few defenders among my peer group. But the result of the confrontation proved the rightness of my attitude of faith and courage in the face of persecution. As I have quipped in the telling of the story – it was *injection* as well as *rejection*, but it injected me with optimism and faith for future trials. And the relating of another such story, though later and more important, will reveal the importance of building upon previous experience.

When I was seventeen years of age, just before national conscription ceased, my call-up papers arrived. I picked up the envelope from the doormat and my heart turned over, because I had thought about it, debated the matter with myself and a few friends, and knew quite clearly what I ought to do. As a Christian, I felt I could have nothing to do with war, and here came the crunch. My parents were moderate socialists, and for them conscription was an evil necessity, and though they did not want their son to join up, they had such respect for authority and such a negative, learned attitude towards 'conchies' that the possibility of refusal did not arise. My Baptist minister had been a chaplain in the RAF (and a good one at that!), and though there has always been a pacifist strain among Baptists, he was personally opposed to conscientious objection, believing that one could 'bear witness' as a serving soldier. None of these attitudes or arguments convinced or moved me, I had to deliberate, reason and come to my own conclusions, and what I came to was this – that despite my parents and clergy influence, despite my friends' attitudes, affirmations or compromises – I knew that I should take a stand. Now what kind of stand? And here came my own kind of compromise. It was clear to me that I could not be a combatant soldier. But not to go at all, to refuse simply and clearly to have anything to do with the system, was a radical step which would put me out on a limb. So as the date of registration drew near, I thought I would register for a non-combatant unit.

The day came, and I went down to the local labour exchange where registration was taking place. In the queue were a few school pals, as apprehensive as I was, but with no clear convictions strong enough to make them take a stand against conscription. I knew some of them had no place for violence or war on humanitarian grounds, but with no Christian faith or the ability to state such a case they could do nothing else but conform.

Eventually I stood at the desk, facing one of the clerks, and the registration began. I gave my name, address, date of birth and so on, and then:

Clerk: For which service do you state a preference?

Me: Oh, RAF I think – but I want to serve in a non-combatant unit.

Clerk: You'll go where you are put.

Me: No, I'm sorry, but I want to serve in a non-combatant unit.

Clerk: We tell you – you don't tell us!

Me: Look, I'm sorry but I *do* feel strongly about this, and I can't go into a combatant unit.

At this, the clerk lost his cool and got edgy–he'd been registering lads all the morning, and probably was fed-up with this repetitive job. There was a queue behind me, and he told me in clear language that I would do what I was told.

Me: No I won't do that. There must be a way to get into a non-combatant unit–what do I have to do?
Clerk: You have to be a conscientious objector.
Me: Well, no one told me that, (turning to the lads in the queue) did you know that?

But no one would look at me directly, let alone answer me. I suddenly felt alone. I need not have felt like that, because if I had maintained my clear conviction, I would have then experienced what came later, an overwhelming sense of God's presence. In a few moments of time, I heard the interior voice which said: 'You see where compromise has led you. If you had done what you knew you ought to do, you would not be in this mess now. But it's not too late–if you will take your stand.' And immediately I knew what I should do, and this 'infusion' of the necessary strength was given. And so:

Me: Look, I've said I'm sorry, but now I know what I should do. Not only will I not serve in a combatant unit, but I will not serve at all. I want to register as an unqualified conscientious objector.

At this point, the clerk really did get angry, for not only was I causing him trouble, but I had been vacillating, and was obviously not going to co-operate or submit to authority. So I carefully but firmly adjusted my attitude, looked directly at him, and said:

Me: I'm not going to sign your form, and unless you register me as a conscientious objector, I am going to leave now.

I remember, quite clearly, the quiet and deliberate manner in which I spoke, and the half-turn I took, though I had butterflies in my tummy. But now there was nothing which could shake me – it was *contra mundum* again, and if the firing squad had been there, I would have maintained my stand. This taught me a great deal about myself, and about what had happened to me over the five years since my conversion. Suddenly the clerk sighed, realised now what he had on his hands, looked squarely at me (did I detect a wry smile), and said:

Clerk: Come back! (Silence). Name please!

And we began again. I left the registration office walking on air. I had actually been 'delivered' from my own compromising inconsistencies – the Lord had actually stepped in, clarified the situation, and enabled me to act decisively and according to my deepest intuitions. I was a pacifist by nature and by conviction, and I had been given the courage to act upon it. But the story did not end there.

That afternoon we were holding one of our beach mission jamborees in which I ordered a double-deck bus, filled it with children and helpers, and headed for one of the Gower beaches – bathing, open-air service, and a general good time of witness, fellowship and fun. I got on the bus and met John, one of the helpers, who said to me: 'How did you get on today? You went to register, didn't you?'

'Oh yes,' I replied, 'it was a bit of a surprise really – I registered as a c.o.'

'Oh, I'm not surprised,' and he grinned, 'I was awake praying for you until four o'clock this morning.' This really bowled me over, and filled me with great joy. There was a network of prayer, of concern, of brotherly love. I know I'm an emotional Celt, but I could have run behind the bus with joy and gratitude. But that wasn't the end.

When I got home, my father said to me: 'Well how did

things go today, son' (He never called me 'son' save in times of particular intimacy or concern.)

'Oh, very well,' I said. 'I registered as a conscientious objector.'

'What!' he cried. But he wasn't really surprised. 'No son of mine will be a conscientious objector. (I was the only son he had.) You'll have to leave home.'

'OK,' I replied, 'then I'll leave home.'

'You'll *not* leave home,' he retorted.

'But you just said I'd have to leave home.'

But he quickly came back with; 'Well, we'll have to see about that.' Then he gave me a lecture about how it was alright for me to go about like the apostles, but I did not have to face people – a son who was a conscientious objector.

My mother's comment was in line: 'Oh, what will the neighbours say?' She could see that I was not overly concerned with the opinion of the neighbours, and she soon went out shopping. When she returned, she said to my father: 'David, the neighbours say that they *expected* him to be a conscientious objector.' So she was quite satisfied. But that wasn't the end.

In three months I had to appear before a court tribunal at Cardiff, with Judge Ernest Evans presiding, and about a dozen conscientious objectors appearing to state their case before him and a jury. I was committed now, and though the euphoric post-registration feelings had somewhat abated, my conviction held, and there was no turning back. I was seventeen and a half, a bit scared, but prepared my statement with thought and prayer. I also had a written testimony from my minister which disagreed with my stand, but affirmed my conviction and sincerity.

One day, soon after my registration, I found myself praying, asking the Lord not to allow the sort of hypothetical question that people often pose to a pacifist: 'Do you have parents/sister? . . . What would happen if an enemy broke into your home and . . .' Suddenly I came across the scripture which spoke exactly to my condition:

> You will be dragged before governors and kings for my sake, to bear testimony before them . . . When they deliver you up, do not be anxious how you are to speak or what you are to say; for what you are to say will be given you in that hour; for it is not you who speak, but the Spirit of your Father speaking through you.[5]

I could now understand how it is that the martyrs could go forth to die, singing. I was no martyr, and I had not been 'dragged' before governors and kings, but I was called upon by a secular state to be trained to fight and kill without question if need be, for the defence of country, territory and political values. I was conscripted to be under orders, to obey without question; not only to surrender my life (which I was willing to do for gospel values), but to maim and kill for queen and country. And that I could not do. And would not do. Those were my feelings then, and though I have a little more understanding of the complexity of the issues, and the greyness of the shades between black and white now, there is no substantial difference in the stance I would take today.

The day of the tribunal came, and I travelled to Cardiff with John, who had supported me in prayer. 'Suppose they put you in prison?' said my father before I went. He understood and was supportive now, though he still would have preferred me to have obeyed the authorities. 'Well, they'll just have to put me in prison,' I replied, 'but I don't expect it will come to that.' I wasn't at all sure that this was true, and I remember thinking that I would not mind a few months' prison experience – here was more than a tinge of 'martyr complex' present.

We assembled in the courtroom and among the few reporters there was a wonderfully energetic and encouraging Quaker lady well into her sixties: 'Good for you,' she said, 'I'll be here praying.' She was obviously a power to be reckoned with in her quiet way. I was about sixth among the dozen or so appearing, and in the witness box I found myself able to answer questions, to state my case with freedom, and to receive courtesy and patience, save for one of the jury who was rebuked by the judge for irrelevant questions. Then came the moment. The very question I had been thinking of before I discovered my coveted scripture was asked. I had said to the Lord: 'Alright, Lord, I'll just do that. I'll not think out any answers, plan any statement more than I've submitted, but trust in your Holy Spirit to speak in and through me.' And with that I had been content.

Judge: Tell me, do you have parents – brothers and sisters?
Me: Yes, parents and one sister.
Judge: Now suppose your home was broken into in time of war. Your parents and sister threatened and beaten. Would you stand by and let it happen?

Here it was. The very question. And my answer was one which fitted exactly the scripture, one which I could not have invented or planned beforehand without incongruity, but one which, if spontaneous, could make clear how I felt, and it certainly impressed Judge Ernest Evans:

Me: I can't tell you, sir, what I would do in such circumstances, but the Christ who stands by me now in this dock will be standing by me then, and he will show me what to do.
Judge: Do you really believe that?
Me: Yes, I do.

And he went on to another question. But that was the turning-point in his mind and in my experience. It was quite clear now that I would be accepted as sincere and a man of conviction. This was all they asked for. I did not object to giving my time and abilities to farming, mining, agriculture or medical work as they directed me, though I did say that I would not join any uniformed organisation connected with the military. So it was that eventually I did an SRN over a period of three years, and this, in turn, opened up my experience still more, and led to greater avenues of joy and service.

Now all that is not so much a story of suffering but joy. But it does illustrate the kind of maturity that develops in having to face demands which could lead to suffering. I did not go to prison, and was not imtimidated or persecuted by the authorities. Indeed, I had greater respect for British fairness as a result of my tribunal than ever before. Britain, unlike certain other countries, could respect sincere conscientious objection. I wonder how things would turn out if conscription were re-introduced in Britain today? This chapter would then take on another dimension of relevance.

If my convictions had led to intimidation, suffering and imprisonment, I trust that my attitude would have remained one of openness, love and positive joy. I have reason to think it would, and certainly in the experience of the Christian Church, persecution led to joy, and martyrdom was frequently the occasion of rejoicing. The early Christians knew that all those who lived godly lives would suffer persecution, and that to suffer *for* Christ was to suffer *with* him, and eventually to reign with him in glory.[6] When the apostles were arrested, persecuted and beaten for the Gospel's sake, they rejoiced that they were worthy to suffer for the sake of the name of Jesus Christ, and they went on preaching.

Maturity and joy in persecution

The most wonderful thing about persecution and suffering in the New Testament is that it does not lead to a ghetto mentality, to hatred, revenge and bitterness, but to joy, openness, forgiveness and maturity. 'Love your enemies,' cried Jesus, 'and pray for those who persecute you.'[7] And he lived out his message unto death, praying for his murderers: 'Father, forgive them; for they know not what they do.' And he engendered the same attitude in his followers, for Stephen, being stoned to death, cried out: 'Lord, do not hold this sin against them.'[8] It was not an expectation of the early believers that they would enter into some pact of plenty, a prosperity covenant of economic growth. If they gave money away they would be poorer, for they were to lay up spiritual treasure in heaven not riches on earth. If they were to follow Christ they would be persecuted and possibly martyred. Listen to St Paul's catalogue of experience:

> As servants of God we commend ourselves in every way: through great endurance, in afflictions, hardships, calamities, beatings, imprisonments, tumults, labours, watching, hunger . . . with far greater labours, far more imprisonments, with countless beatings, and often near death. Five times I have received at the hands of the Jews the forty lashes, less one. Three times I have been beaten with rods; once I was stoned. Three times I have been shipwrecked; a night and a day I have been adrift at sea; on frequent journeys, in danger from rivers, danger with robbers . . . in toil and hardship, through many a sleepless night, in hunger and thirst, often without food in cold and exposure . . . We were so utterly, unbearably crushed that we despaired of life itself.[9]

The sufferings were real and expected, but so was the grace, the courage, the victory, the joy. It becomes clear in reading the New Testament that the constant expectation of the early Church was persecution, that there should be no surprise or questioning when this happened, for it was of the nature of the fallenness of man that he should persecute the community of love, and it was of the nature of the community of love that it should suffer, forgive, and thereby enter into life and joy, bringing its persecutors with it. And in any case, the Lord had said it would be so, and the apostolic warnings were clear enough.[10]

I sometimes wonder, when I see the 'Christian aerobics' of an evangelical crowd in these charismatic days, how many of them would stand were such persecution to break out again.

And lest I should sound partisan (for I often join in such dancing), when I participate in beautiful and ordered liturgical worship, I sometimes remind myself that Jesus was not crucified on an altar between two candles, but on a cross between two thieves! The fact is that a persecuted Church is a faithful Church, for as Tertullian said: 'The blood of the martyrs is the seed of the Church.' If and when the Church in our country suffers state persecution again (as it does in totalitarian parts of our continent), then God's people will be purified, and a faithful remnant will emerge. If believers are able to love and forgive in the midst of persecution, then God will be glorified and joy will blaze out in the midst of suffering. I have already commented on the tremendous infectious joy and vitality that mark the persecuted Church of the Acts of the Apostles and the whole of the New Testament. But it doesn't stop there. A reading of Church history and a wider awareness of the contemporary Church in persecuted countries communicate the same cruelty and the same joy evidenced in persecutors and persecuted to the present day.[11]

But always there is the awareness of the crucified and risen Lord upholding and sustaining. He does not deliver his people *from* suffering and persecution, but he suffers *with* them, and strengthens them in their sufferings. Such sufferings are viewed from a New Testament perspective in the Epistle to the Hebrews:

> Some were tortured, refusing to accept release, that they might rise again to a better life. Others suffered mocking and scourging, and even chains and imprisonment. They were stoned, they were sawn in two, they were killed with the sword; they went about in skins of sheep and goats, destitute, afflicted, ill-treated – of whom the world was not worthy – wandering over deserts and mountains, and in dens and caves of the earth.[12]

From an apocalyptic perspective they are portrayed:

> Then one of the elders addressed me, saying, 'Who are these, clothed in white robes, and whence have they come?' I said to him, 'Sir, you know.' And he said to me, 'These are they who have come out of the great tribulation; they have washed their robes and made them white in the blood of the Lamb. Therefore they are before the throne of God, and serve him day and night within his temple; and he who sits upon the throne will shelter them with his presence. They shall hunger no more, neither thirst any more; the sun shall not strike them, nor any scorching heat. For the Lamb in the midst of the throne will be their shepherd, and he will guide them to springs of living water; and God will wipe away every tear from their eyes.'[13]

From the annals of Tacitus, who was certainly no Christian, we read:

> Mockery of every sort was added to their deaths. Covered with the skins of beasts, they were torn by dogs and perished, or were nailed to the crosses, or were doomed to the flames and burnt, to serve as a nightly illumination when daylight had expired. Nero offered his gardens for the spectacle, and was exhibiting a show in the circus, while he mingled with the people in the dress of a charioteer or stood aloft in a car.[14]

Some of the early martyrs went singing to their deaths. Some longed for martyrdom as did Ignatius of Antioch, and it does seem that frequently they were immune to threats, tortures and sufferings. The day of martyrdom became known as the martyr's 'birthday', and at the martyrdom of the great Bishop Polycarp of Smyrna in his 86th year, the eleven heroes of Philadelphia

> were so torn with lashes that the inward veins and arteries were visible, so that the very bystanders had pity and wept.

> But they themselves uttered neither cry nor groan, thus proving to us all that at that hour the martyrs of Christ, though tortured, were absent from the flesh, or rather, that the Lord was standing by and conversing with them.[15]

Cyprian, the Bishop of Carthage, who himself became a martyr, exhorted and extolled the martyrs of his day, crying with them:

> Earth is shut against us, but heaven is opened; death overtakes us, but immortality follows; the world recedes, but Paradise receives. What honour, what peace, what joy, to shut our eyes on the world and men, and open them on the face of God and His Christ! Oh, short and blessed voyage![16]

Ignatius, in a celebrated passage, invites the sufferings, so assured is he of the attainment to Christ and heaven:

> Come fire, and cross, and grapplings with wild beasts, cuttings and manglings, wrenchings of bones, breaking of limbs, crushing of my whole body, come cruel tortures of the devil to assail me. Only be it mine to attain unto Jesus Christ.[17]

The glory of all this is not in the sufferings which they endured, for men have suffered for all manner of causes, good and evil, but in their heartfelt devotion to Christ, and in the forgivenesss and love that filled their hearts. Martyrs are not always immune to their physical and mental suffering, either in the early Church or in our own days. But even in pain, darkness and loneliness they are able to enter into the sorrow of God and find in him strength for their fainting hearts, courage to face their trials, and the amazing ability to love and forgive their tormentors.

Perhaps forgiveness is one of the greatest signs of maturity, for it includes understanding and discernment, and is free from revenge and hatred. There is certainly tremendous joy in forgiving and in being forgiven. Forgiveness is full of compassion, so that suffering is transmuted into sympathy and love. Such maturity is the ripe fruit of the Spirit, and one of the most saintly men of our days encapsulates this spirit in his poem from a Gestapo concentration camp prison, entitled 'Christians and Unbelievers':

> Men go to God when they are sore bestead,
> Pray to him for succour, for his peace, for bread,
> For mercy for them sick, sinning or dead;
> All men do so, Christian and unbelieving.
>
> Men go to God when he is sore bestead,
> Find him poor and scorned, without shelter or bread,
> Whelmed under weight of the wicked, the weak, the dead:
> Christians stand by God in his hour of grieving.
>
> God goeth to every man when sore bestead,
> Feedeth body and spirit with his bread,
> For Christian, heathens alike he hangeth dead:
> And both alike forgiving.[18]

Notes

1 Harold S. Kushner, *When Bad Things Happen to Good People* (London: Pan Books), pp. 10f.
2 2 Samuel 12:19–23.
3 Kushner, *op. cit.*, p. 140.
4 Richard Lamerton, *East End Doc* (Cambridge: Lutterworth). See, for example the chapter 'Care of Dying Cockneys'.
5 Matthew 10:18–20.
6 2 Timothy 2:12; 3:12; Acts 5:41.
7 Matthew 5:24.
8 Luke 23:34; Acts 7:60.

9 2 Corinthians 6:4f.; 11:23–27; 1:8f.

10 See 1 Peter 4:1, 12, 13; Matthew 20:23; 1 Peter 2:21–25.

11 See H. B. Workman, *Persecution in the Early Church* (London: Charles H. Kelly), and especially for a contemporary understanding, the publications and work of Keston College on specialised studies of religion in communist countries.

12 Hebrews 11:35–39.

13 Revelation 7:13–17.

14 *Ann*. xv. 44. Workman, *op. cit.*

15 *Mart*. Polyc. 2. Workman, *op. cit.*

16 *de Exhort. Mart*. 13. Workman, *op. cit.*

17 *Ig. Eph. 1*. Workman, *op. cit.*

18 Dietrich Bonhoeffer, *Letters and Papers from Prison* (London: Collins Fontana), p. 174.

7 Joy: Personal and Corporate

Joy integral to personal and corporate life

I have always found two powerful forces within me, both of which are important to my sanity and maturity, and both of which contribute to the fulness of life. They are solitude and community. I am not speaking of loneliness and company, of simply being alone and being with a crowd. For many people loneliness is the personal hell of their lives – it savours of isolation, alienation, and ultimately death. To others, being in a crowd does not alleviate their isolation, and it is no solace to be part of a mass of people, all of whom are intent on their own tasks, their own goals, their own relationships.

When I speak of solitude and community, I mean the solitude which is the positive space for the integration of all one's interior faculties to produce creativity and joy, and the community which allows inter-relationships to take place between individuals and small groups, with the larger merging within the fulness of the great community of love – which the Church is meant to be in its celebratory and mystical dimensions. The 'communion of saints' is the fulness of the personal and the corporate.

The joy of the personal

For me, it is necessary first of all to affirm the personal. To be myself, to 'enjoy' myself, allowing full play to all the creative, imaginative, intelligent and physical faculties that I possess. I have interior resources which are more than I even imagine, let alone describe. When I am alone, at the times when solitude, as distinct from loneliness, is given free reign, then I can laugh and sing, I can rhyme and dance, I can walk, run, and put my body, mind and heart to work with the free play of all the creative faculties which are mine by virtue of my humanity. Now all this sounds somewhat romantic and vague, but perhaps it would help if I made it concrete. Let me describe the first part of a day recalled from my six months of personal solitude on the very edge of the Lleyn Peninsula 1983–84.

I wake a little after 4.00 a.m. on a dark, autumn morning, in the small stone cottage, to the thudding sound of the sea which heaves and swells on three sides of the peninsula, and to a stiff morning breeze blowing over from the Irish Sea. I get up in the darkness, and wrapping a blanket around me, light the candle in front of the icon of Christ. I do my ablutions, limber up to get my circulation going and my joints loosened up, then settle down on my prayer stool, with good posture, straight back, relaxed body, letting go all tensions, and with slow belly-breathing, invoke the name and power of the Holy Trinity dwelling within me, from whom all inspiration and creativity comes. Sometimes I just stay there in the stillness for as long as the Spirit indicates, but usually, after a few minutes, I take up the night office of hymns, psalms and readings, which lasts, with the silence following, up to about an hour.

Then, in the awareness of the indwelling Spirit, I sense the direction of my day – the variation is great, and the mood alternates between ecstatic joy and a certain quiet melancholy, with all shades between. There is no need to put on a mask, to project an image, to put my best foot forward, for there is nobody to impress, nobody to cheer, nobody to instruct, encourage or berate! I am simply and solely myself – myself in God – God in myself – and there is only the world of darkness, wind, sea and sky to relate to, interpret, and co-operate with.

I make myself a cup of coffee, then put on my running shoes and set off over the mountain for a half-hour run, primarily to get warm, and seconadarily to keep fit. The cold, fresh breeze upon my face, the smell of the salt, the prickly feel of the gorse, the crying of the mountain sheep and the thudding of the sea combine to lift my spirit to the Lord – for the Lord not only resides in the interior cave of my heart, but is high and lifted up, and immanently indwells his creation.

I jog along the mountain path and feel the texture of the earth and grass beneath my feet. I find myself a little breathless, and after ten minutes or so catch a glimpse of the two small islands *Ynys Gwylan Fach* and *Ynys Gwylan Fawr*, to the south of the peninsula out in Cardigan Bay. Then, rounding the corner under the dim sky and over Bardsey Sound I lift up my eyes and suddenly the dark and menacing beauty of Bardsey Island comes into view. I lie down on the mountain grass cropped by the sheep, and look up into the lightening sky, and sigh for the restlessness within my heart, which is caused by the profound awareness of my solitude with God, and by the absence of my Lord. Written down like that it hardly makes sense, but it is the story of love which is given and received, yet which has not reached its fulness, but awakens desire and longing in the heart of the lover.

On such a morning, on such a mountain, in such solitude, my aloneness is sheer joy, and yet I feel at a far deeper level a solidarity with our common humanity. I think of those I love, and who love me, and cry a little for them. When I use the term 'joy' in this respect it does not mean 'happiness' – indeed it is not incompatible with a certain melancholy. Joy runs deeper than pleasure or pain – and I don't think I could claim to be 'happy', though joy is within. Sometimes it runs as a deep and quiet stream beneath my varying moods of melancholy and heaviness, and sometimes it bubbles up to be manifested in exuberance and vitality.

I quickly get cold, so get to my feet again and run around the path, over the rocky top sheep track which looks down into Caernarfon Bay, completing the circular run back to the cottage. I put the kettle on, wash in the luxury of warm water, and have some thick, sticky porridge and coffee. This brings me to (sometimes) a glorious sunrise, or (sometimes) the rising of a stiff wind, but in any case to the beginning of another day of solitude which will lead me into a deeper experience and another dimension of my communion with God.

Such writing is a kind of shorthand to me, for I know something of what I mean, but perhaps I should try to spell it out a little more closely, if it is to be communicated. One of the primary reasons for my seeking and being driven into solitude is love. All my life I have sighed and longed to enter into the fulness of love, and hardly knew, for many years, what I was seeking. Of course, love was to be sought and found in its fulness only in God, and I knew a little of what Augustine meant when he wrote: 'You have made us for yourself, and our heart is restless until it rests in you.' But although I found God's love mediated in scripture, in church, in sacraments, in human relationships, and most of all in human love and creativity, yet my heart was searching for a deeper, closer, more mystical and intimate bond of love, and this I felt at its most profound when I was alone. This was enhanced when the aloneness was in a place of beauty, and especially at such times as the rising and setting of the sun or the opening and closing of the year – places and times of promise, hope, yearning and glimpsed fulfilment.

And as I felt the longing at its most profound in solitude, so in my experience the glimpses which were vouchsafed to me were usually imparted at such times when I was alone. I found I could feel, intuit, know and apprehend the presence and touches of God more clearly, more intimately, more immediately in solitude than when distracted by the commerce of relationships, however creative and productive they were in various ways. In solitude my yearning was deeper, my seeking more direct, my loving both more intense and more tranquil than when with others. So strongly do I feel these things that I cannot but believe that my desire for solitude contains within it the essence of call and vocation, though how that will eventually work out I do not know. I am not merely led, but driven;[1] I do not merely see, but search; love is not just a choice, but an integral part of my life – indeed my goal and end. It is no mere platonic 'flight of the alone to the Alone', for I am not more alone in solitude than is God in the communion of the Holy Trinity. My roots are not only within the earth, in the very stuff of creation, but also sunk deeply within the common soil of our humanity. I am part of a species, in solidarity with my fellows, and by that very fact, a priest of creation, poised between heaven and earth, participating in both humanity and divinity.

Among the writings which have jumped out at me at their very first reading and have accompanied me down the years, is a poem which I found among the treasures of the *Oxford Book of English Mystical Verse*. It is by Augusta Theodosia Drane, a Carmelite nun, and is an exposition of lines from St John of the Cross. One of the reasons why it has so attracted and held me is because of the nature of her mystical quest – the strange mystical beauty that haunts her nights and days, that calls and teases her with its mysterious loveliness, and yet the 'thing itself' is never spelled out – only he who knows can understand, and only he who has found can ever seek. It is called 'What the Soul Desires', and is impossible to quote piecemeal, so I reproduce it in full:

There Thou wilt show me what my soul desired;
There Thou wilt give at once, O my Life,
what Thou gavest me the other day!
(St John of the Cross)

There is a rapture that my soul desires,
There is a something that I cannot name;
I know not after what my soul aspires,
Nor guess from whence the restless longing came;
But ever from my childhood have I felt it,
In all things beautiful and all things gay,
And ever has its gentle, unseen presence
Fallen, like a shadow-cloud, across my way.

It is the melody of all sweet music,
In all fair forms it is the hidden grace;
In all I love, a something tht escapes me,
Flies my pursuit, and ever veils its face.
I see it in the woodland's summer beauty,
I hear it in the breathing of the air;
I stretch my hands to feel for it, and grasp it,
But ah! too well I know, it is not there.

In sunset-hours, when all the earth is golden,
And rosy clouds are hastening to the west,
I catch a waving gleam, and then 'tis vanished,
And the old longing once more fills my breast.
It is not pain, although the fire consumes me,
Bound up with memories of my happiest years;
It steals into my deepest joys – O mystery!
It mingles, too, with all my saddest tears.

Once, only once, there rose the heavy curtain,
The clouds rolled back, and for too brief a space
I drank in joy as from a living fountain,
And seemed to gaze upon it, face to face:
But of that day and hour who shall venture
With lips untouched by seraph's fire to tell?
I saw Thee, O my Life! I heard, I touched Thee –
Then o'er my soul once more the darkness fell.

The darkness fell, and all the glory vanished;
I strove to call it back, but all in vain:
O rapture! to have seen it for a moment!
O anguish! that it never came again!
That lightning-flash of joy that seemed eternal,
Was it indeed but wandering fancy's dream?
Ah, surely no! that day the heavens opened,
And on my soul there fell a golden gleam.

O Thou, my Life, give me what then Thou gavest!
No angel vision do I ask to see,
I seek no ecstasy of mystic rapture,
Naught, naught, my Lord, my Life, but only Thee!
That golden gleam hath purged my sight, revealing,
In the fair ray reflected from above,
Thyself, beyond all sight, beyond all feeling,
The hidden Beauty, and the hidden Love.

As the hart panteth for the water-brooks,
And seeks the shades whence cooling fountains burst;
Even so for Thee, O Lord, my spirit fainteth,
Thyself alone hath power to quench its thirst.
Give me what then Thou gavest, for I seek it
No longer in Thy creatures, as of old;
I strive no more to grasp the empty shadow,
The secret of my life is found and told!

The Joy of the corporate

I have always known, within my own being, the tension between solitude and company, the personal and the communal. Primitive man understood much more than we do, the sense of what we now call 'corporate personality'. He was part of a family, a group, a clan, a tribe. These were social and religious units which expressed solidarity, union, communion, belonging. And out of such primitive societies and cultures there arose seers, gurus, prophets who held within themselves a sense of the corporate, so that they could represent the whole people.

The Bible makes much of this sense of solidarity, for the whole race is found 'in Adam', the faithful are 'in Abraham', and one of the most precious theological and existential insights of the New Testament, especially in St Paul, is that the believer personally, and the Church corporately, are 'in

Christ'.[2] John Donne, as a poet as well as a theological preacher, knew that no man is an island, and as a consequence, he says: 'Any man's death diminishes me, because I am involved in mankind; and therefore never send to know for whom the bell tolls; it tolls for thee.'

It is perhaps because I feel the tension so sharply that I am able to feel both poles of solitude and community. I have made clear my desire for solitude, my love of aloneness, the precious joy of finding that place, geographically and existentially, where I am alone. Perhaps that is why I also appreciate the joy of community, a profound sense of the corporate. Paradoxically it is when I am most alone that I feel the deepest sense of the corporate. Often, being with a crowd gives me a superficial sense of belonging – and it takes solitude and silence for me to really affirm my solidarity with the race. It is when I am alone that I can truly feel that I am 'in Adam' – that is, a human being with all the pain and glory that this implies. But it is also then that I can affirm that I am 'in Christ', part of the wholeness of the communion of saints in heaven and earth.

One of the symptoms of psychic disease is the inability to reciprocate joyfully, to share, to listen to others and maintain true dialogue with one's brothers and sisters. One of the primary questions I have to ask in making my solitude experiments and taking off into the wilderness, is whether the basic thrust of such an exercise is negative or positive. If there is an inordinate element of escapism in the attitude that leads a man into the wilderness, it needs to be evaluated objectively, not only by himself, but by his community, his peer group or whoever is taking responsibility for his spiritual and mental welfare. This is why requests to a community-chapter or council from one of its members to test a vocation to solitude must not only be taken seriously, but there must also be undertaken a psychic as well as a spiritual evaluation of the brother or sister's vocation and pilgrimage. A man must be able not only to live in community and social interaction with other's, but must be able to hold together the tensions of solitude and community. He must be aware of the communal nature of the Church, and see himself as part of the wholeness of Christ's Body, manifesting one vocation which is incomplete without the sharing of fellowship, service and compassion in the world.

I am not writing this book or this chapter for would-be hermits, but for ordinary Christians, part-sanctified but redeemed sinners! The same lessons have to be learned by all believers who value their personal lives of depth, difference and individuality, for they are the same people who have to relate in a communal and gregarious manner in the Church and in the world. Far from it being a burden or a negative discipline, the matter of 'getting things together' in terms of the personal and the communal should be a joy. To live in the joy of solitude and to share the blessings of communal fellowship are both gifts of God – and in varying degrees we are all called upon to discern the basic pattern of our own lives, neither becoming frenetically active or destructively introvert. Some of us need more fellowship for our spiritual growth and evolution in grace, others of us need more solitude, and if we get the mix wrong, then we shall know frustration in different forms. I meet professional people (inside and outside the Church), whose frantic activism hides the hollow emptiness of their souls, and they run around committees, make plans and ceaselessly activate others to hide an interior poverty that comes to light when they suffer a heart attack or some such affliction prematurely. In any case, if they are fortunate enough to reach their seventies without physical or mental breakdown, they will have to face the loneliness of death, and that will be a moment of reckoning. But then I also meet people who use religion and spirituality to escape from responsible and mature life and action in the world. Their spirituality and discipline are more Platonic than Christian, and they make a nature/grace dichotomy which holds 'spiritual' things as good and 'material' things as evil – these are certainly not biblical roots. Thomas Merton sounds a warning:

> Under the pretext that what is 'within' is in fact real, spiritual, supernatural, etc., one cultivates neglect and contempt for the 'external' as worldly, sensual, material and opposed to grace. This is bad theology and bad asceticism. In fact it is bad in every respect, because instead of accepting reality as it is, we reject it in order to explore some perfect realm of abstract ideals which in fact has no reality at all. Very often the inertia and repugnance which characterize the so-called 'spiritual life' of many Christians could perhaps be cured by a simple respect for the concrete realities of every-day life, for nature, for the body, for one's work, one's friends, one's surroundings, etc. A false supernaturalism which imagines that 'the supernatural' is a kind of Platonic realm of abstract essences totally apart from and opposed to the concrete world of nature, offers no real support to a genuine life of meditation and prayer. Meditation has no point and no reality unless it is firmly rooted in *life*. Without such roots it can produce nothing but the ashen fruits of disgust, *acedia*, and even morbid and degenerate introversion, masochism, dolorism, negation.[3]

Both personal and corporate

It is not a case of either/or, but both/and. It is not that Christians must be extrovert, outgoing, gregarious, continually and solely expressing devotion and worship in corporate acts and meetings. Neither is it that one's faith is a solitary, individualistic and private matter, with no social and communal dimension and implication. Of course there are vocations within the Church catholic which call some to active, public and community service in the Church and the world; and there are also contemplative vocations which call others to ministries of prayer and adoration with varying degrees of solitude. But generally, the Christian lives a mixed life, with a mixture of solitude and community, of activity and solitude, and the total neglect of either is destructive.

The truth is that often the man called to solitude is the one who is not only capable of communication, but who rejoices to proclaim and share the love of Christ which overflows his heart and mind. The story of solitaries is frequently one in which they had to move further and further into the desert, either because there were too many people wanting to receive their ministry of evangelism and healing, or else there were others whose hearts drew them into solitude, and they gravitated towards the man who evidently lived in the immense silence and mystery of God. This was certainly true of Antony who is reckoned to be the father of hermits, whose story was told by the great Athanasius. In contemporary times it was also true of Thomas Merton. His heart longed for solitude, but he felt tremendous tensions within himself, being so gregarious and loving to communicate on spiritual, aesthetic and academic levels. Contrary to popular opinion, Merton only made three journeys outside his monastery. He was a stable monk for twenty-seven years in one monastic community, and during the latter years spent much time in his hermitage in the woods around the Abbey of Gethsemane in Kentucky. But if he did not go out to people, they came to him. His Cistercian brother, John Eudes Bamberger, writes of him:

> . . . There was a steady stream of persons of multifarious interests coming to speak with him from all over the world. He counted among his friends Vietnamese Buddhists, Hindu monks, Japanese Zen-masters, Sufi mystics, professors of religion and mysticism from Jerusalem's University, French philosophers, artists and poets from Europe, South America and the States, Arabic scholars, Mexican sociologists and many others. He was not only at home with all these men, he was on most friendly terms with each, and anyone who has been at the informal

meetings he held with them over the years recognised how much pleasure he took in such company.[4]

Not only is the joy of communication evident in these words describing Merton, but by his willingness to dwell deep within the heart of God, he was able to share the fruits of his contemplation. The man called into the wilderness, into the way of solitary prayer, is called there for the Church and for the world. He is not accumulating merit to save his own soul – he realises that his salvation is in Christ, apart from human merit – a free gift of matchless grace. But he is there in order to enter into both the joy and dread of being truly human. He is there to plumb the depths of his own humanity in the light of the Spirit of God. He is there to be exposed to the divine fire and the divine love – both the judgment and the mercy of God. He is there to descend into the abyss of his own being, which leads to the abyss of the mystery of God's being.

This leads to a solidarity of sharing, a new burden and gift of intercession, and a new confrontation with the powers of darkness. In such a dark night Jacob wrestled with the angel, and it is in the darkness of silence that the man of prayer enters into an ever-deepening union with God, on behalf of the Church and the world. It is God's will for his image and likeness to be perfectly restored in our humanity, and in Jesus, the new Adam, we are made new. The man of prayer lays aside all distractions in his search for the restoration of the divine image, and the Spirit of God works within such a man to regenerate, indwell, elevate and restore our poor humanity, so that it may reflect again the divine image.

This is no individualistic quest, though it is an intensely personal one for all who participate. It is a quest of the solitary as part of the Body of Christ, and it is the quest of the whole Church, reflected in its members. The sad truth about the world, the Church and individuals, is disintegration and brokenness, and the call is into a unity and communion with

God which heals such brokenness and restores communion and community at every level.

Living it out

Talk is easy and words are cheap. The world has heard the incessant chatter of both its politicians and theologians, and looks for the reality to be expressed in concrete manifestations of individuals and communities living together in harmony, compassion and healing. Now where are such people and places to be found? All sorts of secular communes, kibbutzim and communities have sprung up during the last three decades. Many of them have failed through human weakness and others because there was no ideology or philosophy of life strong enough to ensure vision, dedication and perseverance. Alongside these, there has been a revival in the concept of community among Christians of all denominations, and some, with no monastic or liturgical background, have been drawn or driven into community life around the Gospel. It was exciting, while living with the Community of the Transfiguration near Edinburgh in the early 1970s, for me to witness the establishing of the Community of Celebration which came out of Graham Pulkington's pastoral and community experience from the Church of the Redeemer in Houston, Texas, an Episcopal parish that opened out in Gospel community life. My experience with this community was during its time of early experimentation on the island of Cumbrae on the west coast of Scotland. What joy it was to have fellowship with a lively community which had regard for liturgy *and* spontaneity, catholic *and* pentecostal worship!

Similar roots gave rise to the Post Green community in Dorset, and fellowship experienced during the annual community days between the Society of St Francis Friary, Post Green Community, Pilsdon Community, The Barnabas Fellowship, and the Sacred Dance Group and others has been enriching and enthusiastic.

It was the influence of the Church of the Redeemer

experience back in 1975 that stimulated serious gospel-community thinking within the small group led by Jim Wallis, which led to the formation of The Sojourners. This group was neither fundamentalist nor social-gospellers. It had a powerful evangelical experience, a Gospel vision and a commitment to a simple and radical life-style that sought to glorify God and help the poor and underprivileged. Its social and political concerns were born directly out of Gospel experiences, and that is why Jim Wallis has emerged as a contemporary Christian who demonstrates in word and deed the integrity that the world looks for in a man dedicated to Christ. After his visit to the Church of the Redeemer and just prior to the founding of The Sojourners, he wrote;

> Our time there convinced us that we had to be as committed to the pastoral dimension of our life as to the prophetic. We came away feeling that both vision and nurture were critical for the survival of any community. Without a gospel vision of justice for the world, community can become ingrown and self-serving; and without nurturing relationships, community does not exist, as we knew only too well. In the fall of 1975, eighteen adults, two babies, a puppy, and a cat moved to Washington to begin a new life together.

I recall, with much joy, the visit I made with Sister Eileen Mary SLG, to the Hutterite (Anabaptist) community at Robertsbridge, East Sussex, some years ago. It continues to flourish and represents the Mennonite/Hutterite/Anabaptist witness, and how impressed I was by the quality of community life, not only to the basic teachings of the Gospel, but to a joyful and simple work ethic and a pacifist witness which comes down from Reformation times. This community, together with its sister communities in Germany and the United States, is the tip of the Anabaptist iceberg, which has a new relevance to Gospel life and vision today.[6]

Within the Society of St Francis we have a special

relationship with the ecumenical 'Jesus-Bruderschaft' community in Hunfelden, West Germany, situated in a beautiful location called appropriately Gnadental (valley of grace), and that community, together with the Taizé Community and the Grandchamp Community in Burgundy, bear witness to the kind of thinking found in Dietrich Bonhoeffer's book *Life Together*, which was written on the eve of World War II, and came out of his thinking and experience as head of the German 'Confessing Church' seminary at Finkenwalde. Writing of solitude he says:

> Let him who cannot be alone beware of community. He will only do harm to himself and to the community. Alone you stood before God when he called you; alone you had to answer that call; alone you had to struggle and pray; and alone you will die and give an account to God. You cannot escape from yourself; for God has singled you out. If you refuse to be alone you are rejecting Christ's call to you, and you can have no part in the community of those who are called.

and of community he says:

> Let him who is not in community beware of being alone. Into the community you were called, the call was not meant for you alone; in the community of the called you bear your cross, you struggle, you pray. You are not alone, even in death, and on the Last Day you will be only one member of the great congregation of Jesus Christ. If you scorn the fellowship of the brethren, you reject the call of Jesus Christ, and thus your solitude can only be hurtful to you.[7]

Bonhoeffer knew the joy and the pain of solitude. He knew also the joy and the pain of community. 'Only as we are within the fellowship can we be alone,' he says, 'and only he that is alone can live in the fellowship.' And both are by the call of Jesus Christ.

Monastic community life in the Roman Catholic and Anglican communions has its many branches, bearing fruit for the healing of the nations, and the different emphases bear witness to the variety and diversity within the Body of Christ – the Benedictine family, Carmelites, Augustinians, Dominicans, Franciscans, Jesuits – monks, nuns, friars, sisters, communities and societies which have a contemplative or active emphasis, with vigorous new life appearing continually, such as the Little Brothers and Sisters of Jesus who possess a gentle, contemplative spirit with a powerful social and political concern, conforming to Gospel simplicity and compassion.

The monastic tradition of the Eastern Churches has not only maintained its primitive communal witness stemming from Pachomius and Basil the monastic founders, but as well as this coenobitic, community life, the eremitic or desert solitary life has persisted down to the present day. The witness and writings of the Desert Fathers of Palestine, Egypt and Syria bear witness to the communal/solitary tradition, and it still remains for someone to draw comparisons and contrasts between this Eastern tradition and the monastic witness of the Celtic Church of our own islands.

From this Orthodox tradition, Metropolitan Antony Bloom brings together personal love for God and love of one's neighbour in a story he tells of a Russian *staretz* (elder) who engaged in a deep life of prayer while having charge of the labourers who worked on the monastery land. He was asked why his workers were diligent and honest while others were lazy and deceitful. He replied that when he gave them their work in the morning he was overcome with pity for them, for many had left their village and family out of economic necessity. Returning to his cell he prayed to the Lord for them: 'Lord, remember Nicholas, he is so young, he has left his new-born child to find work because they are so poor he has no other means of supporting it. Think of him and protect him from evil thoughts. Think of her and be her defender.'

So he began to pray, and as he felt the presence of God more and more powerfully, he reached the point where he could no longer think of anything on earth. Worldly things vanished, and

God alone remained. Nicholas, his wife, his child, his village, his poverty were all lost in God. Then deep in God he felt the divine love which contained all those for whom he prayed. The torrent of the divine love carried him deeper into God, then back to earth again and his intercessions and to Nicholas. Then it happened again – God's presence became stronger, earth receded, and he was carried again into the depths where God's love contained all things. Such powerful encounter with God, detachment from self, and immersion in the divine love is, for Antony Bloom, the fundamental character of intercession.[8]

One of the great charismatic characters of the Orthodox tradition is Symeon the New Theologian (949–1022), the greatest of the Byzantine mystics, whose theology is full of light and glory. He spoke of the communion of saints as a golden chain bound together in the light and love of the Holy Trinity. He writes of indissoluble union with God which is the quest of the soul consummated in Christ. Here there is no individualism, though the experience is intensely personal, and it is caught up in the mystical glory of being found in the heavenly Adam in whom all humanity finds its salvation and glory:

> He was suddenly completely there,
> united with me in an ineffable manner,
> joined to me in an unspeakable way
> and immersed in me without mixing
> as the fire melds one with the iron,
> and the light with the crystal.
>
> And he made me as though I were all fire,
> And he showed me myself as light
> and I became that which before I saw
> and I had contemplated only from afar.

I do not know how to express to you
the paradox of this manner.
For I was unable to know
and I still now do not know
how he entered, how he united himself with me
and with whom I was united?

I shudder and I fear lest,
if I tell you, you will doubt,
and you will fall into blasphemy
because of your ignorance of such an experience,
and you may even lose your soul, my brother.

Nevertheless, having become one being,
I and he to whom I was united,
how shall I call myself?
God, having two natures, is one person;
he has made me a double being.[9]

From such heights of mystical glory I have to come down from the mountain and face the ordinary self that I am, and the ordinary community to which I belong, with all the difficulties and joys involved. As one brother said to me, 'It ain't easy,' and those words reflect the patience, openness and charity that is required to affirm gospel values in living together. I remember hearing as a young Christian at the Keswick Convention, the stories of missionaries who were filled with vision and enthusiasm to spread the Gospel, but when they got to their overseas mission station, they found it almost impossible to live with the contrary creatures who were their fellow-missionaries on the field! Now I understand what that means because I live in community. It is something that is not experienced in the often unreal 'fellowship' of church gatherings, mass rallies and weeks of concentrated evangelism or ministry–and this applies as much to Catholic as to Evangelical groupings.

But there is also joy to be recorded. There have been times when I have had to exercise great self-control during liturgical prayer or a solemn mass when I have wanted to dance and sing for joy (it isn't always appropriate). And there have been times when I have found myself in tears with brothers and sisters within our community – and tears mean joy as well as sorrow. I belong to the Franciscan family, and the three notes of our Order are humility, love and joy. *The Principles* sound these notes:

> The chiefest of all forms of service that the brothers and sisters can offer must ever be the effort to show others in his beauty and power the Christ who is the inspiration and joy of their own lives. They will seek to do this, not in a spirit of aggression, nor with contempt for the beliefs of others, but rather because, knowing in their own experience the power of Christ to save from sin and to give newness of life, they must seek to share their own supreme treasure. Out of the fullness, therefore, of devoted love they would seek to give their beloved Master to all.[10]

To love Christ, to live Christ, to share Christ . . . these are things which call forth the dedication and enthusiasm of the personal and the corporate. I find the reciprocal relationship of the solitary and the communal parts of myself a thing of great joy, though not without tension. I have noted elsewhere that one of the great weeks of my life was the time spent in St David's, Wales, in the autumn of 1975 at the gathering of brothers and sisters around the theme of the solitary life. The reverberations of that week remain with me now and have orientated my heart towards solitude and prayer. The maturity, humour and transparent singleness of heart which were manifested indicated that these were people who knew what they were about, though they did not profess to have fully attained.

In *Solitude and Communion*, the published selection of papers from that week, Fr Roland Wallis included an appendix on

'Communal Solitude' commending the *skete* form of Christian community, in which a group of solitaries would gather around an *abba* or father for counsel and training. Each monk had his separate cell, often out of sight and sound of his neighbour, and most of the time was spent in solitude. 'There was also simple accommodation for visitors,' says Fr Roland, 'of whom they often had more than they wanted!' At the end of the article he quotes Fr Augustine Baker who affirms that the supreme life of vision and union with God is not reserved for such solitaries or monastics, but is open to all God's people. '*All* will arrive at the top of the mountain,' says Fr Roland, and goes on with the quotation with which I shall close this chapter:

> It is an illustrious proof of the abundant, most communicative, overflowing riches of the divine goodness to all His servants whatsoever that in truth of heart seek Him, that this state of contemplation . . . should neither be enclosed only in caverns, rocks, or deserts, nor fixed to solitary religious communities, nor appropriated to the subtlety of wit, profoundest of judgement, gifts of learning or study, etc.; but that the poorest, simplest soul living in the world, and following the common life of good Christians there, if she will faithfully correspond to the internal light afforded her by God's Spirit, may as securely, yea, and sometimes more speedily, arrive to the top of the mountain of vision than the most learned doctors, the most profoundly wise men, yea, the most . . . confined hermits.[11]

Notes

1 Cf. being 'led' in Matthew 4:1 with being 'driven' in Mark 1:12

2 See 1 Corinthians 15:22,45; Galatians 3:7, 29; Hebrews 7:9; 1 Corinthians 5:17, Galatians 1:22.

3 Thomas Merton, *Contemplative Prayer* (New York: Doubleday), pp. 38f.

4 *Cistercian Studies*, Vol. 1, 1981, pp. 34f.

5 The story of Jim Wallis' pilgrimage and his radical call to gospel conversion is told in *The Call to Conversion*, and *The New Radical* (Tring: Lion Publishing).

6 A cursory glance at their periodical *The Plough* indicates the breadth of their theological and practical witness, with articles on personal commitment to Christ, evangelism, nuclear warfare, children and education, community life, prison ministry, poverty and racial justice.

7 Dietrich Bonhoeffer, *Life Together* (London: SCM), pp. 57f.

8 See *The Essence of Prayer* (London: Darton, Longman and Todd), pp. 344f.

9 *Hymns of Divine Love*

10 *The Principles*, 22.

11 *Solitude and Communion*, p. 82.

8 A Contemplative Perspective

Retrospect and prospect

If a contemplative perspective is developed as part of the life of prayer, then at different times, words like retrospective, introspective and prospective become part of an ongoing process of dynamic and interior evaluation. We look back in gratitude, we look within in simple trust and we look forward with anticipation – but all from the vantage point of a contemplative perspective. The word perspective may be translated 'looking through', and it indicates for the believer a basic trust in the providence of God who in all things works together for good with those who love him.

The outcome of such a perspective is the joy of living in what has been called 'the sacrament of the present moment.' This involves a deliverance from the oppression of the past and the worry of the future. It is not only that mortal man must not boast of tomorrow as the rich fool vainly tried to do[1], but also that there should be an attitude of complete trust in the providential care of our heavenly Father: 'Seek first his kingdom and his righteousness, and all these things shall be yours as well. Therefore do not be anxious about tomorrow, for tomorrow will be anxious for itself. Let the day's own trouble be sufficient for the day.'[2]

From the simplicity of Brother Lawrence's *The Practice of the Presence of God* to De Caussade's *Abandonment of the Divine Providence*, the biblical and desert witness to the power of living in the present moment is preserved. It is the immediate, conscious and loving awareness of the *now* – that God is here *now*, is at work *now*, and that the believer may rest in his love, giving all things into his hands. This is the contemplative perspective in action, a 'seeing through' the materialistic and temporal covetousness of this world. It means leaping into the freedom and joy of possessing nothing, of letting go not only possessions, but ambition, attachment to intellectual or emotional relations, so that one is utterly free and utterly available to God. It is the perspective of faith, the gazing into eternity, the simple trust which looks to God alone in the present moment and trusts him implicitly come rain or shine, come pain or gladness, come life or death, for it rests in the divine will. And this is perfect joy.

Yet in a strange way this sacrament of the present moment includes the dimensions of retrospect and prospect. When there is an immediate trust in God, then faith becomes totally inclusive:

> How good is the God we adore,
> Our faithful, unchangeable Friend;
> His love is as great as his power
> And knows neither measure nor end.
>
> 'Tis Jesus, the First and the Last,
> Whose Spirit shall guide us safe home;
> We'll praise him for all that is past,
> And trust him for all that's to come!

The retrospective view is not one of bondage, guilt, oppression, and failure, but a recitation of the faithfulness of God, who up to this time has been faithful. A contemplative, retrospective view means that the pattern of providential leading can be traced, the thread can be perceived, the pattern established. This is usually not possible prospectively – from the vantage point of the present, the future cannot be forecast, for faith has a certain 'unknowing' about it. But the believing heart can look *back*, and say: 'Ah yes, I see how that in all my perplexities and in spite of all my failures, the Lord was gently guiding, overruling and causing all things to work together for good.'

It was impossible for Joseph to believe that his brothers' hatred was for the greater good. When he fell into the disused pit, was sold into Egyptian slavery, languished in the prison cell – these things did not seem to fulfil any greater, much less divine, purpose. But looking back in contemplative retrospect, he could declare himself to his astonished brothers: 'I am your brother, Joseph, whom you sold into Egypt. And now do not be distressed, or angry with yourselves . . . for God sent me before you to preserve life.' And again: 'You meant evil against me; but God meant it for good'[3] The prospective contemplative dreams of Joseph as a youth were fulfilled, but only in retrospect did the pattern become plain:

With mercy and with judgment
My web of time he wove;
And aye, the dews of sorrow
Were lustred by his love.
I'll bless the hand that guided,
I'll bless the heart that planned,
When throned where glory dwelleth,
In Emmanuel's land.

There is a particular joy experienced in looking back with gratitude. It is a place for tears and rejoicing; the realisation that not only our weak faith and our poor failures, but even our sins are taken up into the divine purpose which cannot fail, for 'he is faithful that promised'. We must not live in the past, or dream of days that used to be; and we should not allow the failures, sins and obsessions of the past to weigh us down. We can rejoice in the faithfulness of God who has begun the good work in us, and who in his forgiving love will complete it.

But then there is the matter of prospect – the future. Again we must not day-dream into the future in either a negative or an inordinately ambitious manner, though there is a place for contemplating prophecy – listening to one's dreams as Joseph did, when they are initiated by God. Joseph found that his prospective dreams indicated the way the Lord would lead him, gave him inward assurance to strengthen him for adversity, and also enlightened him for his own and others' good on the course of his pilgrimage. When he lay in the pit, was dragged along the Egyptian road, or ministered to the prisoners in the round tower, his prospective dreams channelled the revelation of God into his heart.

In this sense, then, we can develop our contemplative perspective in 'seeing through' the pain and adversity of the present, into the glory that is to come. Such faith-vision and affirmation strengthen us for the present conflict and sustains us to continue in the path of faith and loving service.

This was the way of Noah when he built the ark with not a cloud in sight; it was the way of Abraham when he left Ur of the Chaldees not knowing where he was to go; it was the way of Moses, hidden as a child, refusing to embrace the court of Egypt, choosing rather to suffer affliction with the people of God. These, and many others, 'endured as seeing him who is invisible.' Their present contemplative faith-vision gave them joy and hope, even though they did not attain the fulness of the promise in this life. These heroes of faith pass before our eyes in the eleventh chapter of the Letter to the Hebrews, and the writer evaluates such a contemplative faith:

> These all died in faith, not having received what was promised, but having seen it and greeted it from afar, and having acknowledged that they were strangers and exiles on the earth. For people who speak thus make it clear that they are seeking a homeland. If they had been thinking of that land from which they had gone out, they would have had opportunity to return. But as it is, they desire a better country, that is, a heavenly one. Therefore God is not ashamed to be called their God, for he has prepared for them a city.[4]

Power for the present

A contemplative perspective, then, enables us to see through the empty claims of this world, through a bondage to past guilt and failure, through present pain or blessings to glimpse the glory of the world to come. But it anchors us, not in past attainments or future ambitions, but in God himself, who is the eternally present One. A true contemplative perspective imparts power in the present strife and pilgrimage, and enables the joy of past blessings and of future glory to shed its fragrance upon the path now – today – in the midst of all the positive and negative factors influencing our journey. The arena of faith necessitates a contemplative perspective, for it is only in God himself that the strength and joy can be found to sustain present discipleship in a world of struggle and darkness:

> Therefore, since we are surrounded by so great a cloud of witnesses, let us also lay aside every weight and sin which clings so closely, and let us run with perseverance the race that is set before us, looking to Jesus the pioneer and perfecter of our faith, who for the joy that was set before him endured the cross, despising the shame, and is seated at the right hand of the throne of God. Consider him who endured from sinners such hostility against himself, so that you may not grow weary or fainthearted.[5]

One day one of our novices was finding the going very hard. Community life can make immense demands upon novices and professed, and joy is often tempered by trials and difficulties in a particular house with its relationships and pressures from which there seems no release. He came and told me how he felt he had lost his vision, was unable to cope with the demands, and could not find the depth of faith that he had valued so much in the past. I told him to climb the steep hill above the friary which looked over thirty miles of rolling country, to get a geographical and spiritual adjustment of *perspective* – this being the operative word. I told him to cry, complain and spill out all his pains and trials to the Lord there, and to allow the Lord to impart to him the perspective of faith. There he would be high above all the petty problems and the real difficulties of the friary below, and he would get a smell and glimpse of the glory of transfiguration. He did that, and it happened! He was renewed in spirit, and with the perspective of eternity he was enabled to return to the struggle below and engage in the joy and difficulties of relationships, reconciliation, prayer and service. Power for the present had come from that contemplative perspective which must be preserved in faith.

Contemplative perspective and Gospel Life

Does a contemplative perspective differ from the Gospel life? This is a primary question for Christians, because if it is *contrary* to the Gospel life then it ought not to be encouraged; if it is *extra* to the Gospel life, then it is superfluous and therefore not needed; if it is *other* than the Gospel life in a neutral sense, there is no time or place for it.

The fact is that the contemplative perspective is universal, in the sense that it is older and more widespread than the Christian tradition. It is the good soil in which the Gospel of Christ can take root and bear fruit, and it is, in any case, part of the Christian tradition itself.

What I am saying is that the contemplative perspective is a basic, human attitude of creativity, openness and love, and if it is absent from the Christian Gospel, then the Gospel itself becomes distorted. The Christian life of prayer is rooted deeply in contemplative soil, as was that of the patriarchs and prophets of the Old Testament. All the great world faiths, including Christianity, have become corrupt (at the same time as there persists a faithful remnant who embody the truth of love). If ever and whenever ideas of temporal power and spiritual totalitarianism reveal themselves, giving rise to the justification of exclusivism and holy war, it is clear that there has been a departure from the contemplative perspective. In order for such doctrines to find support, the contemplative dimension must be denied, for bad religion soon gives rise to political and materialistic greed, and a lust for spiritual and temporal power.

This is clear in the attitude of the Desert Fathers of the fourth century in Palestine, Syria and Egypt. When the Christian Church was declared acceptable and established by the decree of Constantine, after his supposed conversion, the Desert Fathers took themselves off into the desert to live out more truly the Christian alternative to political and established religion. Thomas Merton wrote about the contemplative perspective of the early Taoists personified in Chuang Tzu of the fourth century BC, and the Desert Father of the fourth century AD, with their common heritage.[6] In *The Way of Chuang Tzu*, he writes:

> I have been a Christian monk for nearly twenty-five years, and inevitably one comes in time to see life from a viewpoint that has been common to solitaries and recluses in all ages and in all cultures. One may dispute the thesis that all monasticism, Christian or non-Christian, is essentially one. I believe that Christian monasticism has obvious characteristics of its own. Nevertheless, there is a monastic outlook which is common to all those who have elected to question the value of a life submitted entirely to arbitrary secular presuppositions, dictated by social convention, and dedicated to the pursuit of temporal satisfactions, which are perhaps only a mirage.

The feel of such a contemplative perspective that Merton finds in Chuang Tzu

> . . . is characteristic of a certain mentality found everywhere in the world, a certain taste for simplicity, for humility, self-effacement, silence, and in general a refusal to take seriously

> the aggressivity, the ambition, the push, and the self-importance which one must display in order to get along in society. This other is a 'way' that prefers not to get anywhere in the world, or even in the field of some supposedly spiritual attainment.[7]

For Chuang Tzu, as for the Gospel, you lose your life to save it, and to seek to save it for one's own sake is to lose it. There is an affirmation of the world that leads to spiritual ruin and loss, but there is a renunciation of the world that leads to spiritual life.

In the introductory essay to *Wisdom of the Desert*, Merton says that the Desert Fathers saw the tragedy of accepting the cross as a sign of temporal power when the Emperor became 'Christian'. They did not believe that a 'Christian state' could exist, for Christianity and politics could never mix to produce a fully Christian society. Such a society was spiritual and extra-mundane, the mystical Body of Christ. Their flight was not negatively individualistic, but they would not allow themselves to be passively ruled by a decadent state. But neither did they place themselves above society. They were not proudly contemptuous of other men in a superior manner. On the contrary, they objected to the division which made the successful impose their will on others who had to surrender and be imposed upon. They refused to be ruled by men, but had no desire to rule themselves. Nor did they run from human fellowship, but affirmed a gentle and wise humanity where all men were equal, and the only authority under God was a charismatic, voluntary authority of wisdom, experience and love.

They were out to live in simplicity and love, to find their true selves in Christ, and in order to do this they rejected the fabrications of social compulsions. Perhaps their challenge to us today is that they represent freedom from an increasingly bureaucratic, herd mentality which seems to be overtaking us. Their joy was in simplicity, a certain economic poverty, a complete lack of aggression, and an affirmation of intuitive humanity. In this way they affirmed a basic, unsophisticated humanity, free from the illusion of power, wealth, territory and political manipulation. For as Merton says:

> What can we gain by sailing to the moon if we are not able to cross the abyss that separates us from ourselves? This is the most important of all voyages of discovery, and without it all the rest are not only useless but disastrous. Proof: the great travellers and colonisers of the Renaissance were, for the most part, men who perhaps were capable of the things they did precisely because they were alienated from themselves. In subjugating primitive worlds they only imposed on them, with the force of cannons, their own confusion and their own alienation.[8]

Gospel roots in contemplative soil

When a worldly and secular society looks at the Church, does it find evidence of the gentle, quiet and open attitude which gives birth to simplicity of life, joy in the common life of our humanity and a sharing of truth in love? A contemplative spirit without the Gospel may be deficient in content, but it does communicate a sincerity and openness in which our humanity can rejoice and grow. But the Gospel without a contemplative spirit becomes a pseudo-gospel, and can lead to exclusivism, authoritarianism and one-upmanship which our Lord will not own.

This sham gospel is not confined to any one section of the professing Church, but is found in exclusive evangelical fundamentalism as well as in authoritarian Catholicism and superior and arrogant orthodoxy. The charismatic movement, which has brought a certain joy and liberty into worship, liturgy and prayer, has also developed, in certain quarters, a frenetic and judgmental ghetto mentality which cannot accept the rich diversity of other traditions, and cannot find the silence and solitude necessary for any man or any church to grow in grace and love.

This leads to the situation where Christians who talk most about joy manifest it least; where the affirmation of assurance is shouted louder to silence the conflict and doubts hidden beneath the superficiality of impoverished devotion. The claim to joy, assurance and freedom is sounded loudly, but it is by their fruits that they shall be known.

A similar thing is true about an arid and scholastic orthodoxy, whether it is of the evangelical or Catholic variety. If joy and enthusiasm are absent, and if there is no stirring of the springs of vitality and spirituality, then correct doctrine is like the sacrifice laid out correctly upon the altar, but the fire of God is absent. I owe much to both the evangelical and the Catholic traditions, and gladly acknowledge the teaching and experience which is part of the wholeness of the Church, but if the contemplative perspective is lacking, then there is no true joy, no true openness, and indeed a denial of that very humanity which our Lord loves and came to save.

Nor am I forgetting the kind of liberal Christianity which is afraid of the personal nature of the evangelical experience and the theological demands of the Catholic tradition. There are many worthy insights and attitudes in the liberal tradition, with a moral and ethical awareness which puts many other Christians to shame. But if this lacks a contemplative dimension, then it can become paralysed because of its own compassion-fatigue. This is a result of a drain on the reservoir of human compassion which does not depend upon the divine sources of love and joy. The liberal tradition can become even more frenetic in its good works than either the evangelical or the Catholic traditions, and the result, in Christians any of these traditions who neglect the contemplative dimension, is a lack of inner integrity and joy. By *integrity* I mean a basic wholeness – an integration of body, mind and spirit that is in touch with the sources of our common humanity. In order for such an integration to take place – and it is a long process – there must be a contemplative life, with its roots of compassion going deep down into God. This produces self-questioning and the facing of a great deal of interior alienation which has to be dealt with in terms of the reconciling Gospel. But it also leads to an awareness of the indwelling Spirit and the integration of all our facilities enabling us to rise to love, joy and peace.

I do not write as a contemplative guru, but as a saved sinner who has been born again into the dimension of the Holy Spirit, within the communion of the Church catholic, and participating in the great contemplative tradition of the Church down through the ages. My contemplative perspective ante-dates my specifically Christian experience – I was contemplative as a child, and converted at twelve years – but the process of integration continues in my life, and gives rise to a greater love, a greater joy and a greater peace, with the passing of time and experience.

Notes

1 Proverbs 27:1; Luke 12:20.
2 Matthew 6:33f.
3 Genesis 45:4f; 50:20.
4 Hebrews 11:13–16.
5 Hebrews 12:1–3.
6 See Thomas Merton, *The Way of Chuang Tzu* (London: George Allen & Unwin); *Way of the Desert* (New York: New Directions).
7 *The Way of Chuang Tzu*, pp. 10, 11.
8 *Way of the Desert*, p. 12.

PART III:

The Experience of Joy

9 Awareness of Spiritual Vitality

Health of body, mind and spirit

Mens sana in corpore sano, a sane mind in a healthy body–that, together with soundness of spirit, is something we should all strive for! It is a tremendous feeling to be caught up in invigorating physical health, by virtue of which you can run, jump, dance, swim–and almost fly! I am not at all sure of the virtue of competitive games, but there is a beauty and exhilaration in teamwork, precision, choreography, which is born of a common discipline, sharing and strenuous training. There is a peculiar joy in the suppleness of the athlete, the swiftness of the runner, the harmony and grace of the swimmer, the speed and energy of the cyclist and the entrancing beauty and charm of the the dancer. What discipline, what spontanaeity, what mind-blowing and scintillating wonder in all these physical things.

Then the mind. A similar sense of wonder and admiration is caught up in areas of intellectual or aesthetic creativity, whether it is the sheer symmetrical beauty of Bertrand Russell's *Principia Mathematica* (or his *History of Western Philosophy* for that matter!), Einstein's genius displayed in his intuitive and intellectual writings, or the application of a simpler mind to any creative task which involves disciplined study and rewards the student with intellectual satisfaction.

Most of us have had such satisfaction of body or mind some time in our lives. Those of us who were never supple, lithe and physically precocious may have had glimpses of aesthetic or intellectual joy, and doors which are closed to some are open to others. Indeed if we are deprived in some area, physical or intellectual, we are often gifted in some other, if only in slight degree. To know this, to feel it to be so, to be appreciated, encouraged and inspired in even one of these areas is to have entered into joy – into the awareness of a certain human vitality.

But what of the vitality of the spirit? There, physical and intellectual dimensions are certainly full of analogy, and spiritual vitality may well be experienced in the areas of the physical and the mental. I have written elsewhere of the simple joys of jogging, but I can enter into the spiritual dimension in childlike tumbling in the sea or in spontaneous dancing before the Lord with or without music. I have never been one for organised sport, though I do feel the tremendous corporate power of those who participate in the teamwork and common shared endeavour involved in many open and competitive sports. I'm sure that spirituality is involved in such physical and psychical participation, though each to his own discipline, whether of body, mind or spirit.

We may not be certain if we are in perfect physical health, or in tip-top intellectual form, but we certainly know it if we feel below par. Of course, it is possible to be fairly healthy though not really fit, but health will not be maintained in an unfit body. Lack of physical or intellectual exercise and practice will soon be felt in an inability to co-ordinate muscles or grey cells in time of need. So with spiritual vitality and energy. There have been times when lack of prayer and the contemplative dimension have led me into the spiritual doldrums, and it is always to do with a basic neglect of my relationship with God. If I am in love, then love will be the mainspring of my motive and will. But there are times when my spiritual muscles become flabby and soft, and I even fail to hear the call within my soul to rise in the ecstasy of adoration or the call to ascetic discipline – and both are part of a healthy and vital soul. Our Franciscan *Principles* has this to say about the matter:

> Without the constant renewal of divine grace the spirit flags, the will is weakened, the conscience grows dull, the mind loses its freshness and even the bodily vigour is impaired. They (the brothers and sisters) must therefore always be on their guard against the constant temptation to let other work encroach upon the hours of prayer, remembering that if they seek in this way to increase the bulk of their activity it can only be at the cost of its true quality and value.[1]

There are times when I am spiritually aware – when the love and mercy of God overflow me, inebriate me or cause me, with no spectacular emotional or affective upheaval, to give myself to vigil prayer, to study, to discipline or works of compassion. There may be no emotional 'high' as a stimulus or reward – but simply the knowledge that this is right and good and true.

As there are times when I have been aware of physical well-being, or intellectual ability and challenge, so there are times of spiritual awareness in which I know, feel and trust in the presence and blessing of God upon my life. There are also times when, without effort, there is a flow, a communication, a contagion of joy and enthusiasm in relation with others who look to me for help, fellowship, vitality or encouragement – all forms of joy. There are times when I cannot put a foot wrong, when all that I say or preach or share or do is signally blessed by God – and there have been times when the opposite has seemed true!

Some of the best memories and experiences of joy are to do with sharing my spiritual life with non-believers. It is difficult to know what to call them – *unbelievers* sounds pejorative; *non-Christians* (though not judgmental) sounds elitist and negative, and I want to cover non-believers of all kinds. There are times when I not only give but receive. Indeed there are times when I am overjoyed by the mutuality in which, with some non-believers, I experience a dimension of the Holy Spirit in which I am constrained to give up all labels and categories and just want to communicate within our common humanity.

On a hitching lift a while ago, a driver asked me if I could tell him, in one sentence, what I stood for. I said I would preface my sentence by saying that it is almost impossible for me to say anything without looking to Jesus who is the centre of my life. But I did say: 'In one sentence, I seek to be open and loving with others on the simple basis of being human.' He was amazed and filled with appreciative joy. I hastened to add that I did not live up to such a quest, but he said that to hear the desire expressed in that way gave him immense hope. I am so often aware that when I share the way that God has led me, people are intrigued, elated and sometimes dumbfounded and spellbound by the pilgrimage I describe. I find myself often amazed by my own pilgrimage, especially when I step back from the immediacy of the daily process of its evolution.

There are times in prayer and quiet when I weep openly before the Lord (though not before others), because of the privation and fulness of the way. There is such a pattern of sorrow and joy, such a depth and height of human awareness that I find myself trembling with the implications of what it can and does mean.

During this time of writing, I am chaplain to our enclosed sisters at Oxford, and between retreats and ministry to groups and guests I am able to get some chapters written. This period has served to underline and emphasise what I have said in the above paragraphs. In last week's Third Order retreat we shared at a level of spirituality and humour a dimension of contemplative prayer which evoked challenge, longing and yearning in some hearts. In corporate sharing and individual ministry I have been involved in intimate joy and pain in other lives. I have been aware of being a channel of love, compassion and spiritual energy, and I have received from those who have been open and honest in their quest.

There have also been periods of sharing with non-believers.

Some of these have asked to come and talk because they saw the ITV *Encounter* documentary of my six months of solitude in North Wales. There have been scores of letters and requests to talk – and a number from those who cannot lay claim to Christian faith or to religious experience as they understand it. The remarkable thing is that their very request and desire seem to me to indicate a longing and quest which can be called religious, for it has a hunger for God and transcendence within it. Sometimes, as during this period, it has been my joy to point out to some of them that there is already an awareness of spiritual vitality within them. As I have gone on talking of my own experience which has wonderfully shed light upon theirs, and as we have mutually shared, communicated, sought elucidation and listened to men and women of faith and prayer, there has been the awareness of something (or someone) sharing with us. There has also been the sharing of secular writings. Just during this week there has been an exploration of the writings of Carl Jung and M. Scott Peck, the neurologist Oliver Sacks, the novelist Herman Hesse with references to many others.

This puts evangelism in a different light – it does not compromise the proclamation of the Gospel, but the emphasis is on sharing and not declaiming. And in any case, I learn from those whose hearts are on the journey of enquiry for I am a fellow-pilgrim, and the mutuality of seeking and learning imparts an openness and dialogue that reveal the dimension of the Holy Spirit.

I am aware of a certain spiritual vitality, enthusiasm and joy. I am also aware that not only *can* it be communicated, but it *is* communicated in love and openness. I am also aware that I have more in common with seeking souls who cannot affirm dogmatic finalisations than with an orthodoxy which is dry and withered on the one hand or which is arrogant, unbending and exclusivist on the other.

There *are* clear teachings in scripture and the great traditions on prayer and contemplation; there *are* assurances of forgiveness, salvation and redemption that can be shared, taught and experienced. But it must all be done in a spirit of humility, love and joy. Only then will the energy be communicated instead of dissipated; only then will the light shine in other hearts and minds and not be lost in darkness and confusion. And out of such shared experience has come the light of discovery and the joy of leading others into hope and a gentle trust in God.

Over the last few years I have produced many pieces of writing for those with whom I share a *soul-friend* relationship, and for novices, retreats, missions and publications. A little while ago I wrote of the hidden treasure of my own spiritual and human quest. I did try to write it for non-believers without God-language and theological jargon, and though, if I had persisted, I *may* have succeeded in doing that, it took a different form and is unlike any other piece of writing that I have produced. I want to reproduce it here because it lends itself to the substance of this chapter. I will include it as I wrote it without further comment, save to say that the brief parables I would write over it are those found in Matthew 13:44, 45:

> The kingdom of heaven is like treasure hidden in a field, which a man found and covered up; then in his joy he goes and sells all that he has and buys the field. Again, the kingdom of heaven is like a merchant in search of fine pearls, who, on finding one pearl of great value, went and sold all that he had and bought it.

The Pearls of Greatest Price

Jesus told the story of the pearl of great price, which exercised such power and fascination, and begot such yearnings in the merchant man that he sold everything he had for its possession. And of the treasure hid in a field: when the labourer had struck it with his spade, he gave all to possess the field for the sake of the treasure.

I think it is like that for me – the pearl, the treasure, is that which is deepest, is highest. It is the discovery of our true self, or at least the intuitive knowledge of its potential existence – and we must remain true to that. It does not matter that we do not yet possess it, have not yet entered into participation and experience of its heights and depths. What matters is that we live in the possibility of such. It does not matter that we have transgressed it, denied it, forsworn it – it sounds again and again, like the sound of that immortal sea from which we come, to which we go.

It is that which moves me, entrances me, inebriates and dazzles me. It is that for which I live and die – its strange beauty sometimes elevates and sometimes humbles me, causing me to hide away from its radiance. But there are times when I am drawn to its dazzling glory, longing to be united with it, lost in its fiery blaze. It is truly me, more myself than I have ever known, and yet more 'other'.

It is more truly myself, and therefore more truly other. The more I seek, yearn, long, imagine and participate in the quest of 'knowing' it, the more I realise that the edges of my individuality are blurred, and that I am carried out, carried away, powerfully, dangerously into that land of immanence – transcendence which speaks of the profound mystery of God.

There have been times when I have wondered if I *could* so trample upon it, deny, quench, insult and alienate myself from it, that it would depart beyond recall. But always, always it has returned without my seeking, for it is not under my control, and inherently manifests this difference from 'magic' which can be possessed, used, manipulated for one's own ends. Then again there have been times when I have wondered if, by my attitude, deeds, and 'other loves' I have blinded, deafened, desensitised myself to its glory and magnetic power. But no, it seems whatever I have done or thought or purposed, somehow it returns, not merely at the edges of my ways, but deep, deep in the profound depths, at the centre of my being, which is another way of saying that I am drawn up into the dazzling and dizzy heights, so that when I read certain stanzas of St John of the Cross, they affirm such longing;

> The more I rose into the height
> More dazzled, blind and lost I spun.
> The greatest conquest ever won
> I won in blindness, like the night.
> Because love urged me on my way
> I gave that mad, blind, reckless leap
> That soared me up so high and steep
> That in the end I seized my prey.

And so I cannot but affirm that I am held, moved, shaken to my very foundations by the divine Love in which I live, move and have my being. Nothing can ultimately deflect me from the divine Love, though I may bargain and cheat, misinterpret and misunderstand, and waste my substance on all kinds of riotous living! There is no place and no one in whom my very soul is satisfied, my very life fulfilled, save in the depths of that eternal Love which has ever sounded within me and will not cease.

Now I cannot affirm all that, with all its implications, for myself alone! Indeed as soon as I move out of mere individualism (which is one of the first great discoveries of 'the Way'), then the corporate nature of the quest becomes clear. There is an inter-relatedness, a close web of encounter, an interpenetration or interpermeation of love and knowledge. This means that the more truly I love myself, so the more seriously I enter into the depths of myself, and find myself in touch with my own depths. In this way I more truly experience the mystery I call God, and become aware of the inclusive nature of such a quest and pilgrimage, which therefore includes all others who are on the way.

And who are those on the way? It seems to me that those are on the way who *know* it to be so, and those who *hope* it to be so, and those who *yearn* for it to be so, and those who cannot, out of humility, believe it to be so, and even those who have no conscious thought of 'a way' but live in openness and love. In short, all are on the way who have not looked into the face of Love and rejected it! And I leave even those to the loving mercy of God.

This is really an affirmation of the greatness of the love of God, and the ultimately irresistible nature of his grace. It amazes me that not all the failures, the brokenness, the alienation, the doublemindedness, the compromise, cowardice and downright perversity of my life disqualify me from Love. And as these things do not *disqualify*, neither do my integrity, sensitivity, creativity, intelligence, wit and ability *admit* me to Love. It is all a gift of grace. I am loved because I am. By token of my creation, I am loved, sustained, held, forgiven, reconciled, because of the amazing overflow of the divine creativity and redeeming love.

So past sin and failure, present compromise and cowardice, and future helplessness, psychic disintegration or even death itself cannot separate me from the love of God in Christ. Ultimately, though much may intervene between times, ultimately I am united to the divine Love by the Holy Spirit. Through much tribulation do we enter the kingdom of God, says scripture, and the way lies through purgation, but on to illumination and union, which repeats its sanctifying process at different levels and dimensions, but into deeper awareness and participation.

None of this leads to antinomianism or licence, for an experiential knowledge or trust in the divine Love can only give rise to responsive love. Positively it releases from guilt, legalism and the bondage of false religion, into the liberty, assurance and peace that is the mark of a man of faith and prayer.

The pattern for all this is the way of Christ, for as he was born of the Holy Spirit, and spent his life gladly in overflowing compassion and loving teaching and example, giving himself in darkness, pain and suffering, so we are called to walk in and with him, the same path, by the power of the same Spirit, to the heart of the Father. And as his life was the planted seed which, being buried, sprung into new life and dynamic, so we are called to live in him, to die with him, to rise in him, as the pattern and prototype of our present and future resurrection.

Another stanza from that poem of St John of the Cross:

> The steeper upward that I flew
> On so vertiginous a quest
> The humbler and more lowly grew
> My spirit, fainting in my breast.
> I said 'None yet can find the way'
> But as my spirit bowed more low,
> Higher and higher did I go
> Till in the end I seized my prey.[2]

It is the pearl of greatest price. And the knowledge, the quest and the end are all in his Love.

Notes

1 *The Principles*, 16.

2 Roy Campbell (trans), *St John of the Cross: Poems* (Harmondsworth: Penguin Books), p. 55.

10 Communicating Joy

The communication of joy must come from one's rich, interior life. There is no communication of sheer, life-giving joy unless it springs up from one's inmost being and overflows:

> Jesus stood up and proclaimed, 'If any one thirst, let him come to me and drink. He who believes in me, as the scripture has said, "Out of his heart shall flow rivers of living water." ' Now this he said about the Spirit, which those who believed in him were to receive.[1]

The word which is used for 'heart' *koilia* in the above text indicates the profound depths of the being, and St John links this interior river of joy with the Spirit's gifts at Pentecost. Such joy communicates. It springs up and overflows, becomes infectious and embraces others and draws them into the sheer delight of sharing gospel joy.

It may not always be clear to the observers who are drawn into the influence of such infectious joy that its source is the healing love of God. Indeed it may not be directly felt to be such by some who experience deep creative joy in life, but every good and wholesome creative thing that brings joy has its roots in God. Speaking of such joy, our Franciscan *Principles* say that the brothers and sisters 'will carry with them an inner secret of happiness and peace which all will feel, if they may not know its source'.[2]

Joy communicated through preaching

Sometimes, when I reflect upon the way I have come, I

think of some of the things I now miss. The Evangelical and Catholic traditions have run together in my experience, and the communication of joy through both these traditions continues. But because the kind of powerful Welsh preaching I heard as a boy is not now as evident as it was, I feel a sense of nostalgia for it.

There are times when I find myself caught up into a kind of glory in the midst of preaching, and I carry the people with me. It becomes a corporate experience of communication in which preacher and people are held in the sheer communicative joy which the Gospel can engender when it is proclaimed with sincerity and zeal, and when the hearts and minds of the people are open to its truth. The old Welsh preachers, especially in their native language, used to 'go into the *hwyl*' – a kind of *extempore* chanting/preaching style which caught up both preacher and congregation in a fervent and responsible appreciation of the Gospel within the sermon. One cannot evaluate it by an objective observation, but participation was of the essence of its nature. The Welsh will say that it can be compared to nothing else on earth, though a similar experience may be called *sobornost* in the Orthodox Church, and I believe it was a manifestation of the fellowship or *koinonia* in the early Church – the communion of the Holy Spirit.

I remember one of the first times I experienced such a communication of joy and wonder. I was about fourteen years of age, and went to a Pentecostal preaching service in Pontardulais, South Wales, one evening. There were about two hundred people in the church, the singing was glorious and the people were warm-hearted, enthusiastic and expectant. The preacher took as his theme the glory of Christ in the Transfiguration, and he carried us along with him to the holy mountain, where we almost saw and heard and felt the presence of the living God.

Such sermons as these could go on for an hour or longer, and we would be thirsting for more. On this occasion, the preacher was about fifteen minutes into his sermon, and he was describing, as if we were there with him, the beauty and glory of the transfigured Christ. Even as I write these words I am carried back to that occasion, and can see him caught up in the glory of those moments, when both Elijah and Moses faded from view, as the splendour of Christ's radiance shone out above the brightness of the sun.[3]

At this point, something of that glory communicated itself both in and through the preacher, as he became the interpreter of the love and splendour of the transfigured Christ, and as he preached he quietly began to weep. It was not an hysterical outburst of emotion, nor a contrived rhetorical technique, but a simple, felt sense of wonder and awe in which he drew his congregation into a living experience of Christ on the mount of transfiguration.

He stumbled, and was unable to go on, and with the whole congregation I bowed my head in reverence and worship. A beautiful, shared stillness took hold of us all, and quietly, here and there, arose the murmuring of prayer and praise, until very gently someone began to sing:

> And crown him Lord of all . . .
> And crown him Lord of all . . .

following which we all raised our heads, and the preacher wonderfully took up the theme, and then came the joy. It was a sense that the Lord had drawn near, or rather had drawn us into an exposure to the divine presence that gave us joy and wonder. I was deeply impressed by the beauty of such an experience which was intensely personal and at the same time truly corporate; it was so embedded in the nature of the mystical, and yet so liberating and joyous. I turned to an old man on the way out, after the service, and said: 'What was that?' 'That, my boy,' he replied, 'that was the Holy Ghost.' Thus I remember such joy communicated; its validity lay not only in the immediacy of the infectious experience and the spontaneous yet controlled elation which I felt, but in the fact that I still remember it with gladness and gratitude to God.

Christ in you

The above story indicates that the joy of Christ may be communicated through preaching, for he is the substance and content of the Gospel, and preaching at its best communicates his living presence, even though the preacher is inadequate or unworthy. 'I was with you in much fear and trembling,' says St Paul the great veteran preacher, missionary, giant of the faith. But his confidence was in God, and his joy was in the Christ-centred message of the Gospel. He makes it quite clear:

> When I came to you, brethren, I did not come proclaiming to you the testimony of God in lofty words or wisdom. For I decided to know nothing among you except Jesus Christ and him crucified. And I was with you in weakness and in much fear and trembling; and my speech and my preaching were not in plausible words of wisdom, but in demonstration of the Spirit and of power, that your faith might not rest in the wisdom of men but in the power of God.[5]

His preaching communicated Christ, and thus communicated joy, and although his estimation of himself is a lowly one, sometimes calling himself chief of sinners, yet he knew that if the joy of Christ is to be communicated it must be in Christ-centred men and women. The joy of Christ is not imprisoned within the covers of a book or to be identified with the formulation of a credal statement, but is incarnated in those who find in Christ their salvation. As he says again, the great mystery and wonder of the Gospel is the indwelling Christ; '. . . to them (believers) God chose to make known how great are the riches of the glory of this mystery, which is *Christ in you*, the hope of glory.'

If the centre of the Gospel is the indwelling Christ, then the hidden Christ will manifest himself. This means that wherever the Church is true to the Gospel, the hidden Christ will make himself known in love, in compassion, in service and in joy. The only 'sign' that Jesus would give his followers was this one: 'By this shall men know that you are my disciples, if you have love for one another.' Eliza Doolittle, in *My Fair Lady*, objects to Professor Higgins' verbosity when she sings to him:

Don't *talk* of stars shining above,
Don't *talk* of love – show me!

Joy is a quality of life that is often projected as an image in certain religious circles, but it is not difficult to see through it. If that evangelical smile is put on to impress outsiders, to win converts, to assure oneself, people will soon realise it – and they do! Certainly, living in a community of any kind, especially in a religious community, the quality of one's life is soon known. Joy cannot be manufactured. But the converse is also true. When there is a manifestation of real joy, then it communicates positively, and has a life-enhancing quality about it. This is indicated in this anonymous poem, 'Christ in You':

Not only by the words you say,
Not only in your thoughts confessed,
But in the most unconscious way
Is Christ expressed.

Is it a beatific smile,
A holy light upon your brow?
Oh no! I felt his presence
When you laughed just now.

To me 'twas not the truth you brought,
To you so clear, to me so dim,
But when you came to me you brought
A sense of him.

And from your eyes he beckons me,
And from your heart his love is shed,
Till I lose sight of you, and see
The Christ instead.

Joy as a Rule of Life

Part of our Anglican Franciscan Rule speaks of the three notes of our Order, humility, love and joy. If these prevail, the work of the Order will be fruitful, but if they are lacking it will be unprofitable and barren. Of course, joy cannot be commanded, and there is little point in including it in a Rule of Life unless there is a spontaneous welling up of the joy which comes from living union with God in Christ. The reason why the Franciscan tradition is so imbued with joy and spontaneity is because it is Christ-centred, and rooted in creation. The joy of nature and of grace reveals itself in the Franciscan life because it is a Gospel life. Joy is not divorced from sorrow and pain, and therefore it is not artificial and not superficial, but springs up from the passion and glory of Jesus. The Rule goes on to say that the joy of Christ abides even in days of darkness and difficulty, giving courage in disappointment, and an inward serenity and confidence in sickness and suffering. Those who possess it, therefore, for the sake of Christ are able to face weakness, contempt, persecution, hardship and frustration, for in their weakness the joy of God's strength is made known.[6]

It is not enought to go out on mission with brown-habited brothers and sisters, strumming guitars and singing Gospel songs. It is not enough to dance in charismatic rallies or to rejoice in the ordered liturgy of a high mass full of light and beauty. Joy must be seen and felt and communicated in the dark places of life, in the midst of day-to-day community life, and in times of sickness, adversity and old age. But here lies the proof of Christian joy. It is not a matter of 'grin and bear it', not a resignation to fate, to encroaching illness or senility and not a rebellious outpouring of anger because of one's personal impotence. The amazing joy of Christ is that its roots are nourished in what seems to be the slime and mud of darkness and doubt. My breath has sometimes been taken away by the quiet and profound joy which has been in evidence in the man or woman who has trodden the valley of the shadow, in sickness or bereavement. This is the kind of joy that communicates and brings life to others.

Having joy written into our Rule of Life causes us to examine the roots of such joy. It is clear that it is not the transient, emotional 'high' that accompanies outward circumstances or passing pleasures. Joy in its Christian, its New Testament sense, has to do with the flow of the life-giving sap of the true vine as it flows into the branches, invigorating the growth, producing foliage and fruit which is made into the wine of gladness that makes glad the heart of man.[7] Jesus promises us that if we abide in him as the branches abide in the vine, then the result will be not only fruitbearing, but communicative joy. 'These things I have spoken to you that my joy may be in you, and that your joy may be full.'

Be of good cheer

The only joy that can be communicated is that which is real, which is experienced. The reason why there is so much perplexity when real problems of suffering, sickness and bereavement overtake some Christians is that they have tended to confuse emotional excitement and natural enthusiasm with the joy of which Jesus speaks. I am not saying that emotion is not part of religion or that enthusiasm is not part of the Christian life. My own human and Christian life has been suffused with both. But I have had to learn, through some bitter experiences of loneliness, darkness and pain, that the roots of joy are in God, and that such joy can be known alone, and with others, in those dark places of human desolation.

Being brought up on the King James (AV) version of the

Bible, and now using many versions in study, teaching and devotions, I often miss the AV language which moulded me in my formative years. This was brought home to me when, during a month-long mission in the Swansea and Brecon diocese in 1983, I preached the mission sermon at Brecon Cathedral on the difference between the superficial joy of the world and the profound and healing joy of Jesus, illustrated in his words (translated in the AV) 'be of good cheer.'

In the morning I had been visiting a school with the local priest, and went to his vicarage for lunch. I am allergic to mushrooms, and his wife had prepared an appetising casserole, abundant with mushrooms, the presence of which I did not detect until I began to eat! I realised too late, but politely said nothing and hoped for the best. That afternoon we had to visit two farms and return to the vicarage for tea before the Cathedral mission service at 7.00 p.m. About an hour after lunch I began to feel queasy, and we got through one farm visit. Then in the car I was violently sick, so that neither my habit or I was fit for public appearance – and I felt awful!

But having been sick, I began to improve – it was then about 5.30 p.m., and by 7.00 p.m. that light-headed and empty feeling that comes with an empty tummy too frail to receive any further food or drink was my experience! In such a state I climbed into the pulpit to preach, with an immense sense of relief from that awful 'mushroom-queasy feeling', and of gratitude to God for the joy of being able to communicate his word. My preaching went like this:

1. '*Son, be of good cheer; thy sins be forgiven thee*' (Matthew 9:2). The man was paralysed. His friends brought him to Jesus, and because of the crowd they climbed up on to the roof, broke up the thatch and let the man down in his pallet before Jesus. Jesus saw right into the man's heart, discerned his psychosomatic condition of sin and sickness, and got to the root of the matter. He did not say: 'Pull yourself together, dear fellow

snap out of it and look on the bright side.' No! 'Be of good cheer' were words of confidence and faith which heralded the forgiving and healing power of Jesus: 'Son . . . thy sins be forgiven thee; arise, and take up thy bed and go into thine house.' Here is the joy of forgiveness.

The paralysed man felt his condition had been diagnosed, his sinfulness had been recognised, his melancholy had been understood, and he heard words of affirmation, of assurance and of salvation. First of all he felt the joy of forgiveness of sins in his heart, and secondly he felt the healing power of Christ coursing through his body. It was a salvation which meant wholeness and restoration. The *good cheer* of Jesus was sheer joy of living, through forgiveness and healing.

2. '*Be of good cheer; it is I; be not afraid*' (Mark 6:50).
Here the situation is altogether different. Great elation had been experienced when Jesus had felt compassion for the crowd of needy people, because he saw them as sheep without a shepherd and his heart went out to them. The result of this was that he shared his love and his teaching with them until it became late and the people were hunrgy. It was then he quietly prayed over some loaves and fishes and gently but miraculously fed the great mass of people, and the disciples were amazed.

After this he sent his disciples across the Lake of Galilee to Bethsaida ahead of him, while he went up into the hills to pray. Night wore on, and some time between three and six in the morning, while the disciples were battling at the oars against a head-wind, he came towards them through the darkness. Suddenly they became aware of the figure seemingly walking on the water. They were terrified and cried out in fear. And across the water, through the early darkness, they heard the familiar but authoritative voice of Jesus: 'Be of good cheer; it is I; be not afraid.' Then he climbed into the boat with them; the wind dropped, and they were dumbfounded!

The symbolism of this story is powerful. Embarking on the

water after an emotional 'high', the disciples were unable to live on mere experience of past emotions when they encountered the cosmic elements of wind and water. From the great mystery of contemplation and transcendence, the Christ comes to where they are, meets them in the very extremity of their impotence, and cries out words of assurance while at the same time bringing them peace and tranquillity by his very presence. Because he is near they have nothing to fear. Their superstitious fear of elemental spirits is conquered by the reverential fear of the Lord, which is the beginning of wisdom. And it is all heralded by his word: 'Be of good cheer.'

3.'*These things have I spoken unto you, that in me ye might have peace. In the world ye shall have tribulation; but be of good cheer; I have overcome the world*' (John 16:33).

The situation has changed again. After some three years of discipleship in the school of Jesus, through joy and pain, through misunderstanding and enlightenment, through brokenness and healing, the disciples are aware that separation is imminent. Jesus is preparing them for persecution, tribulation, loneliness and desolation. He shows them clearly that the path he walks must be their pilgrimage too, and that by intimate fellowship and union with him they will find peace and victory.

He does not promise them, as some modern evangelists do, happiness, economic prosperity, self-fulfilment and instant tranquility. Rather he pictures this world as one in which the righteous suffer, and love is crucified. But there is no doubt about the ultimate outcome – victory remains with love, and through the tribulation, pain and dereliction, the peace and joy of God will sustain the believer, in spite of external circumstances, and in the face of the worst that the world can do. These words of Jesus on the eve of his passion and death sound over a suffering world today, giving assurance of the ultimate sovereignty of love:

> Behold the hour cometh, yea, is now come, that ye shall be scattered every man to his own, and shall leave me alone: and yet I am not alone, because the Father is with me. These things I have spoken unto you, that in me ye might have peace. In the world ye shall have tribulation; but be of good cheer; I have overcome the world.

The operative word of assurance which the evangelists use in these three texts is *tharseo*, rendered 'good cheer' in the AV, and in other versions, 'have courage', 'take heart', 'have confidence'. It is a word of joy in the midst of sickness, perplexity, fear and persecution. It is a word which heralds Christ's healing, saving, delivering power in the face of all the world's attacks–proclaiming victory even over death itself.

My preaching that evening was out of the experience of weakness and prayer, but joy was communicated because it was based on the simplicity of childlike trust and confidence, and therefore the consequence was a joy felt and shared.

A theology that communicates

Towards the end of my first six months of solitude on the Lleyn Peninsula in 1983–84, the mountain was invaded by a small party of young people climbing one spring Sunday morning. I had lived in solitude during the winter months, but now spring was in the air, and with it heavily-booted walkers would explore the mountain paths. What, at this point, seemed to be an accidental meeting, turned out to be a joyous communication of theology and human sharing. The incident was one of such joy that I recorded it in my journal, so the details are quite precise.

After the celebration of the Sunday eucharist, I had some breakfast, took my bundle of names for intercession and set off to walk over the cliffs, down to the sea, walking, praying and stopping frequently to play a hymn of praise or intercession on my recorder for those who were held in prayer in my heart and mind. Climbing back up the steep mountain path, I lay upon the ground for a time and then began to play:

> Jesus, how lovely you are,
> You are so gentle, so pure and kind;
> You shine like the morning star,
> Jesus, how lovely you are.

Then I became aware of the group of young people on the pathway higher up, leading to my cottage. I stayed where I was for a while and eventually made my way up to the higher path. A friendly, hairy dog came bounding towards me, followed by its owner who grinned at me, and there behind her were her friends. We exchanged greetings, and one of them asked if I was living in the cottage along the way. I said I was, and they began to enthuse about it, confessing that they had sneaked up to the window and looked in, and had seen the little altar-table with its icon of *Christ Pantokrator*, the Almighty, and an open Bible. It was clear that friendliness was in the air, and questions, answers and comments were exchanged. We talked about the Lleyn Peninsula, about holy places, about a sense of the presence of God, and of dark powers in and around this place, and of the early monastic communities and the earlier pagan influences. There were six or seven of them, and one of them, a fellow in his thirties, asked if he might take a photograph of the cottage as he wanted very much to paint it, and painting from a photograph was one of his methods. He did not have his camera with him and he would need to climb the mountain again later in that day with it. We talked about hermits and the life of prayer, and they laughed at my humour over their intrustion into my six months' solitude! I said that Bob could return and take his photograph, and after some more sharing about prayer, meditation and the beauty and awesome bleakness of the surroundings, the group went on its way.

Later in the day, Bob appeared at the front of the cottage, and obviously was not going to disturb me. But I spotted him and offered him a cup of coffee, so we spent a profitable time sharing our understanding of life and its experiences. He confessed that he was not a professional artist, but an avid amateur, and was a plainclothes policeman who investigated frauds. I told him he had come to the right place, and with that kind of openness and humour which is part of the sheer joy of human sharing, we talked of faith and prayer, of violence and love in our poor world. Bob said that he was not a Christian and could not cope with organised religion, but was deeply aware of the beauty and wonder of the natural world. I shared some of my reading with him, and talked of the way in which beauty, art, poetry, music and all things creative can lead to a profound awareness of the mystery of God. He was so wanting to hear more and to share from his experience that we got on famously.

We shared the problems of speaking spatially about God, how he could not be imprisoned in a church building or confined to any particular holy place or space. He listened with excitement when I said that God was 'no-where', was not limited to physical dimensions and that any talk of God in terms of geographical location or in any physical sense was language which belonged to analogy, and was not literal. Bob was immediately interested and said that this was just how he felt, and that he could not believe in a God who was 'man to the *nth* degree', a sort of super-man 'up there' or 'out there', playing cosmic chess with our world and moving the pawns upon the board.

So we went on to talk of finding the mystery of God, of 'presence' in the depth of one's heart, in the world of natural beauty, in the fellowship and inspiration of all creative disciplines, and in all relationships of compassion and love. Wherever men, women and children are open and receptive to love, there is an experience which can interpret and communicate the mystery of God.

And then evil. We talked of the world political situation (I heard a run-down of the news on Sundays so was fairly up-to-date), and of the darkness and violence which manifest themselves at so many levels in our poor world. Bob was a police officer and I was a friar, and we both spoke of our own darkness and ambiguities, and the pain and sorrow we felt at the world's darkness. He spoke of the Middle East situation and of the sadness of Beirut and Lebanon which was in the forefront of the news at that time.

Then, going back to the two books by Fritjof Capra which we had mentioned earlier, we skimmed through the chapter headings of *The Turning Point*. Capra commends a holistic approach to all the great disciplines, including the natural sciences, medicine, psychology, economics, political science and ecology, as well as his own discipline of physics. He points to the new awareness and possibility of transformation in intellectual and intuitive approach, and sounds a clear warning that unless there arises a new dynamic interplay between scientific analysis and mystical intuition leading to a cultural revolution of spiritual openness, then world-wide catastrophe is upon us.

We chatted a little longer, and shook hands with great appreciation of each other's awareness, and he took his camera and bounded up the mountain path to photograph the Peninsula from the top of Anelog, tucking into his pocket the quotation which I had given him:

> After a time of decay comes the turning point. The powerful light that has been banished returns. There is movement, but it is not brought about by force . . . The movement is natural, arising spontaneously. For this reason the transformation of the old becomes easy. The old is discarded and the new is introduced. Both measures accord with the time; therefore no harm results.[8]

I turned back to my solitude, glanced at the icon of *Christ Pantocrator* and the Bible open at the Gospel of the day, 'Jesus the Healer', and commended Bob, his family and friends to the Lord. This communication and rapport which was so real and life-giving imparted joy to us both – in very different circumstances. The meeting was unplanned and spontaneous, and the joy was infectious! He went back to his investigations in the fraud squad, nursing those secret yearnings for all that I represented in my solitude, and I entered more deeply into that solitude, carrying all he represented into the silence and love of God.

Communication as a continuing joy

It is three years since that experience, and having just written that last paragraph I was bringing this chapter to an end, when suddenly a letter arrived from Bob. He had seen an interview on Midlands TV in which I talked about prayer in the middle of a magazine programme. As a result he contacted me, visiting me here at Glasshampton, and delivered a beautiful painting of the little stone cottage where we had met, and we are now continuing what is proving to be a continuation of communicative friendship. And so it goes on.

Notes

1 John 7:38.
2 *The Principles*, 28.
3 Matthew 17:1–8; Mark 9:2–8; Luke 9:28–36.
4 Colossians 1:27.
5 1 Corinthians 2:1–5.
6 *The Principles*, 29.
7 John 15:1–11; Psalm 104:15.
8 Capra's quotations from the *I Ching*, *The Turning Point*, p. vii.

11 Joy in Life and Death

Our people die well

Does it seem strange to include a chapter on death in a book on joy? From the outset, I was persuaded that it is impossible to write about joy without the awareness of sorrow, pain suffering and death. And this is not only because of honesty and integrity – for life is a mingling of joy and sorrows – but also because I am able to affirm the primacy of joy. Joy is basic, and to drink of the springs of humanity is to drink of the springs of joy. And joy continues, flowing as the river of God throughout our lives, and ultimately into the ocean of God's eternal love. Death is not the last word, for joy converts the enemy death into our sister who is welcomed after the long pilgrimage of earthly life.

One of the happy consequences of living in the awareness of the mystery of God from a child is that of the integration of Christian teaching with my own human experience. Although I realised the melancholy sadness of death (for I had a puppy who had fits and died when I was about ten years old), nevertheless I intuited that the melancholy of death was a prelude to another dimension of life in the spirit.

I remember about that time seeing a picture in a large gilt frame which portrayed death in such a way as to lift my heart in joy. It showed a deathbed scene full of glory! An old man with white hair and beard was sitting propped up in bed with pillows, but his arms were extended, his eyes lifted heavenwards, and a shaft of light fell upon his face, irradiating it with beauty and anticipation. His friends were kneeling and standing about the bed in prayer, and the caption under the picture read: 'A Methodist Death Bed'. So impressed was I by that picture, and so much did it accord with my own child-like understanding of Christian death, that it has stayed with me over the years. When I later read that John Wesley said, 'Our people die well,' I remembered the picture and almost laughed with joy. The early Methodists not only had assurance of sins forgiven and the awareness of the indwelling Holy Spirit, but they lived in anticipation of future glory, and joy overflowed into the experience of death, carrying the believer into heaven.

In the Society of St Francis, the professed brothers are encouraged, as part of their preparation for death, to leave written instructions which include arrangements for the burial service. The first time I experienced the burial of a person without a coffin was when our Brother Adrian was laid on a board in his habit, and lowered into the grave we had dug for him in our friars' cemetery in Dorset. He was buried with song and prayer, with procession and incense, with a requiem mass and great rejoicing. As I think of my own death, not knowing how it will come, I incorporate thoughts of dying into my meditation, and plan for the elements of rejoicing I would like to include in the service. I go back to that picture of 'A Methodist Death Bed', wanting to die as well as that old man, with the sunlight of heaven on my face and in my heart.

As well as the Russian 'Contakion of the Departed',[1] I would want included one of Charles Wesley's hymns for a departed believer. Sung to the Welsh tune *Trewen*, even now it fills my heart with joy and gladness, and with the glory which is native to the Christian when thinking of death as the entrance into life, and into the nearer presence of his beloved Lord Jesus. Here it is:

Rejoice for a brother deceased,
  Our loss is his infinite gain;
A soul out of prison released,
  And freed from its bodily chain:

With songs let us follow his flight,
  And mount with his spirit above,
Escaped to the mansions of light,
  And lodged in the Eden of love.

Our brother the haven hath gained,
  Out-flying the tempest and wind,
His rest he hath sooner obtained,
  And left his companions behind,
Still tossed on a sea of distress
  Hard toiling to make the blest shore,
Where all is assurance and peace,
  And sorrow and sin are no more.

There all the ship's company meet
  Who sailed with the Saviour beneath,
With shouting each other they greet,
  And triumph o'er trouble and death:
The voyage of life's at an end,
  The mortal affliction is past;
The age that in heaven they spend,
  For ever and ever shall last.[2]

The theology undergirding that hymn is distinctively Wesleyan, but as the Wesley brothers would be first and quick to point out, basically and joyfully Christian. Stanza one strikes the nearer, loving presence of his Lord after laying aside the burden of the flesh. For the Wesleys, the body is a prison not because it is evil (they were not Gnostics!), but because of its finitude and mortality.

The second stanza brings before us the appropriate analogy of the ship, after its storm-tossed and labouring journey on the ocean of life, entering at last into the heavenly harbour where sorrow and sin are over and a great welcome awaits it. This is the same hope that is expressed by the apostle Paul when he says: 'The time of my departure has come. I have fought the good fight, I have finished the course, I have kept the faith . . .'

As I have pointed out elsewhere, one of the meanings of the word departure (*analusis*) in common usage was the 'letting-go' of the mooring ropes of a ship, so that it can set sail out of the earthly harbour into the waters of the open sea. For Wesley, the analogy carries the ship into the waters of eternity and into the heavenly harbour of love.

If the second stanza indicates a little of the sorrow of the 'companions left behind', the third re-echoes the shouts of joy in heaven where 'all the ship's company meet'. What a wonderful way of describing the communion of saints! As I write these words, it makes me want to be present at my own funeral, to sing the hymn and rejoice in the intoxication of such a theology which shouts with joy in the face of death, and praises the Saviour who will bring all the ship's company home at last. My theology certainly allows for the departed soul to be aware of the joy of a believer's funeral, for as Moses and Elijah conversed with Jesus concerning the manner of his death (the word is *exodus*), on the holy mountain, then why should we not be able to share in the rejoicing of a believer who has entered triumphantly, by grace alone, into the loving presence of his Lord?

Taking grief seriously

Now lest it be thought that I am not taking sickness and death seriously, or looking into the malicious and ugly face of death as it frequently appears to us, let me say that there is a sense in which death is the enemy – though an enemy which will itself be destroyed.[3] I have been present at the death-beds of adults in my medical and priestly work, and though suffering is often more obvious among the bereaved than with the patient, nevertheless there have been times of great sadness and distress with dying people, especially among those who have taken no thought of preparation for the journey we must all make. I affirm all the joy and rejoicing spoken of in the first paragraphs of this chapter, but the other side of the coin is the acceptance of grief and pain in the loss of a loved one for whom one should and must grieve, as Jesus grieved and wept at the grave of Lazarus. I think of a Pentecostal woman who felt it her duty to rejoice at the death of her mother, and who, some months later, suffered psychiatric depression because she had not allowed her grief to manifest itself. Grief repressed gives rise to dangerous symptoms for the person concerned and for all around. I may be wrong in thinking that the Celtic peoples are healthier in this respect than the Anglo-Saxons, but whatever the truth is about that, my meaning is clear. It is healthy to be able to laugh and cry, to sing and mourn, to allow emotion overt expression in the high and the deep places of our human life. I remember standing with a distraught man in Cardiff, looking at the body of his wife, lying in her coffin in his home. She had been under psychiatric care, and had pleaded with him to let her go for a walk by herself, because she was under his constant surveillance, and felt smothered and trapped by such supervision. One evening she persuaded him to let her go out alone, so reluctantly he let her go, telling her to be back in an hour. She did not return, and after an all-night search she was found dead in the early hours of the morning in a park on the other side of the city. As I stood with him he wept and cried out in his sorrow for her dying, and because of his feeling of negligence. I did not attempt to silence him or to assure him that everything was alright. It wasn't. Neither did I need to escape from the embarrassment of a weeping man before the corpse of his wife. He needed to weep, and he needed me to share his weeping and grief. And only then could he begin to hear the necessarily few words of assurance and consolation from the minister of God. It was not a time for words, but for sharing, for grief and for compassion.

I am also aware that it is not only the facts of personal and family grief and bereavement that face us here, but the awareness of a wider grief, cruelty, suffering, torture and bloodshed presented before our eyes and to our hearts daily via the mass media, from all parts of the world. What are we to make of it all – how can we talk of joy in the face of such accumulated suffering – and can *anything* make up for such carnage, torture and violence? I believe that there is strong reason to listen to the words of St Paul when he says: 'I consider that the sufferings of this present time are not worth comparing with the glory that is to be revealed to us . . .'[4] But we cannot help feeling that he did not know what we know, after the holocaust, either of the depth of man's inhumanity to man, nor the breadth of the extent of horrific and refined cruelty in our contemporary world. I believe that Paul realised, more than we do, the depths to which man can sink, though he could not have known the universal practical application of such suffering that we can and do inflict upon each other in these days.

Later today we hope to join with other ecumenical Christians at a mass of penitence at St George's Church, Worcester, which begins a week of vigil for peace – for tomorrow is 6th August, the day on which we celebrate the Transfiguration of Christ, and remember that fateful day in 1945 when the first atomic bomb was dropped on Hiroshima, ushering in a new epoch of nuclear fear for the whole world.

All such violence, cruelty, warfare and bloodshed are death-dealing, and Christians must take it seriously, showing themselves to be people of reconciliation and compassion in a violent world. They must work by life and word for disarmament and peace, even if it means losing their material possessions, standard of living, and life itself. Easy words, but such is the crisis and the challenge today, for whatever position one holds in regard to nuclear weapons and disarmament, it must cause any heart touched with love of Christ to sorrow and weep for the sins of the world.

In the face of all this, endeavouring to take grief and suffering seriously, and looking into the face of death, how can there be room for joy? Can Christian theology and experience make any sense of the sad reality of the absurdity of human life and the apparent meaningless of our existence in the world today?

Life, death and the world to come

The answer to these questions lies in the wholeness of the Christian tradition. It draws not only upon the revelation of God in scripture, but in the living and continuous experience of the people of God down through the ages, including our own days. We have already noted the experiences of Christians under persecution and torture – we have heard the song of the martyrs and witnessed the triumph of the suffering Church under pain of death. Christians of this calibre would say that if there was no world to come, if this life was the only one, and if there was no judgment and justice and no consummation of love in the life to come – even then there would be no life to be lived but the Christian life, and no death to die but a Christian death. For in life and in death the promise of Christ's love and presence is validated to those who launch out into the deep waters of daring faith.

Christians do not live Christian lives or die Christian deaths in order to deserve, earn or merit eternal life. If our lives are to be lived in the experience of forgiveness and compassion, then whether that results in productive fruitfulness or in persecution and death, that is still the way to live. For what is the point of money, ambition, territory, authority and power, if it is purchased at the price of human blood, and in any case ends in death? The Christian does not love Christ for fear of hell or for hope of heaven, but just because of love. And if that love ends in death, then so be it – but love he will!

Let's be quite clear. The Christian hope is not 'pie in the sky when you die', it is rather the loving reality of Christ's forgiveness, compassion and presence here and now. And all such compassion must be channelled toward the alleviation of human suffering and the promotion of forgiveness, reconciliation and peace among people and nations. So even if death is the end, there is still abundant purpose and meaning in life – and in death. Better to die in love and compassion possessing nothing and devoid of power, than to die having amassed wealth, territory, power and reputation, if one's hands are stained with blood. For as my mother once acutely observed: 'there are no pockets in shrouds!'

But having said all that, it is impossible for me to think that Christian life and the experience of God's love is limited to this life. St Paul says in a tremendous chapter on death and resurrection: 'If for this life only we have hoped in Christ, we are of all men to be pitied,'[5] and then he goes on to speak of the risen life of Jesus and of our life in him. The fact is that the whole Christian tradition down through the ages (saving the historical and contemporary heretical sects and the vague liberals who are always with us) has affirmed life and love in Christ for today – and for ever. Eternal life may be qualitative in its basic meaning, but it certainly has no end. Once brought into the saving and forgiving love of Christ, the river of such love flows on into eternity, and into the blessedness of a dimension in God which sorrow and sighing shall be no more, tears shall be wiped from every eye, and in which we shall gaze upon the face of God in glory, and be joined to him by the Holy Spirit of love.

This is no 'reward' for deeds or merit – we have none. It is the manifestation of God's free and loving grace towards undeserving sinners – and it is freely offered to all. Such grace does not make us immune from suffering, deprivation, persecution, pain and death in this life – indeed the Christian may suffer *more* than the unbeliever, and lose everything in the world – but it does sustain the suffering believer with inward peace and joy, even in humiliation, suffering and death. 'In the world you shall have tribulation,' said Jesus on the eve of his torture and crucifixion, 'but be of good cheer, for I have overcome the world.' Who was he to offer such comfort, when he was taken, beaten, tortured and crucified to death? But that's the very point – 'God was in Christ, reconciling the world to himself.' It was Love himself upon the cross for us, suffering *with* the world, dying *for* the world, but rising in power, glory and joy, in order that he might reconcile all things and people to the Father in ultimate joy at the last.

This brings us to the borders of a consideration of Eternal Joy, but before we embark on that, let us look at the attitude of the believer in the experience of death, and try to understand why it was possible for St Francis to call death 'sister death' and to embrace it with peace and joy, though blind and worn out in his earthly pilgrimage.

Human survival and near-death experience

Christians have not usually looked for 'proofs of survival' in terms of *post-mortem* evidence, and orthodox Christianity has always looked askance, or with suspicion, at societies for psychical or parapsychological research, even though these have often been sponsored from within firmly-based Christian commitment. There are areas of spiritualistic and psychic practices which are charlatan, and some which are dangerous, and we have been content to warn Christians against 'dabbling' lest they be infected!

The Protestant tradition has been most fearful and vulnerable because of the dearth of teaching and experience in this area. The Catholic tradition has a greater sense of the communion of saints, offices of prayers and anointing for the dying, of requiem eucharist and prayers for the departed, which make the theology and practice of the faith much richer, and thereby it does not become prey to occult, spiritualistic and mediumistic charlatanism or heresy.

But new things have been happening, and respectable scientific and pastoral research has been brought to bear upon the area of the terminally ill, and modern resuscitation methods have brought to light evidence of survival and experience beyond clinical death. I have to be cautious here, for I am not speaking of scientific proof of survival of death, but of important medically recorded experiences of persons who have 'died' and have undergone resuscitation. For those who want to read up the evidence, I would refer them to the writings of Dr Elisabeth Kübler-Ross, Dr Raymond Moody and others[6] who are physicians of high standing with no theological axe to grind. There are many reseach papers and books from many other quarters in an increasing number, but it is worth mentioning Dr Maurice Rawlings, who writes from the Evangelical tradition, paying great attention to the matter of cardiopulmonary resuscitation (CPR) which he describes in detail, including an appendix on its practice for ordinary people in cases of emergency.[7]

It is not my intention to quote widely from such sources to support or buttress theological considerations, because from within the Evangelical and Catholic traditions I do not believe we need, or should look for, such proofs or support for theological assertions, which are in the realm of faith anyway. But neither do I believe that we should ignore clear and objective evidence from unbiased and reputable medical and psychiatric practitioners. Therefore, although I found much to stimulate thought in Dr Maurice Rawlings' book *Beyond Death's Door*, and found the CPR appendix absorbingly interesting, I did find him subjective in his evaluation, and commend his book with a certain caution.

The point I want to make is that through modern resuscitation techniques, an increasing number of people have reported startling descriptions of immediate 'life-beyond' experiences, after which the patient no longer has any fear of death. The CPR technique involves mouth-to-mouth ventilation for the patient, while at the same time maintaining his heartbeat by compression, until he can recover his own functions. The definition of the 'clinically dead' has now had to be reassessed, for over the past decade or two increasing numbers of people have been resuscitated, who previously would not have recovered apart from the procedure. The technique is now so widespread in medical circles and so recommended in industrial and first-aid procedures that it is continually giving rise to greater interest from every side. The technique is easy to understand, not difficult to practise, and though I would initiate such treatment in an emergency, I am not as convinced as Maurice Rawlings that it ought to be commended on such a scale. I am thinking primarily of the area of geriatric terminal care – but in any case this is outside our present concern.[8]

Complete model experience

There is an increasing interest in the phenomenon of death in the medical and psychiatric professions and in the secular world. Case reports of return after clinical death now run into thousands, for as Dr Raymond Moody says: 'I am now uncovering new cases of this phenomenon so rapidly that I am no longer keeping track of the exact number.' He goes on to say that on the basis of the research work of many physcians and surgeons the question will soon be not whether there really is such a phenomenon of survival after clinical death, but rather what are we to make of it? There is an abundance of testimony of particular experiences of the dying and 'out-of-the-body' experiences in the books mentioned for those who want to examine such witness. We have no time to review such evidence here, but it is worth reproducing the theoretically complete model experience which Dr Raymond Moody constructed on the basis of his case histories. It embodies all the *common* elements of typical near-death experiences:

> A man is dying and, as he reaches the point of greatest physical distress, he hears himself pronounced dead by his doctor. He begins to hear an uncomfortable noise, a loud ringing or buzzing, and at the same time feels himself moving very rapidly through a long tunnel. After this he suddenly finds himself outside of his own physical body, but still in the immediate physical environment, and he sees his own body from a distance, as though he is a spectator. He watches the resuscitation attempt from this unusual vantage point and is in a state of emotional upheaval.
>
> After a while, he collects himself and becomes more accustomed to his odd condition. He notices that he still has

> a 'body,' but one of a very different nature and with very different powers from the physical body he has left behind. Soon other things begin to happen. Others come to meet and to help him. He glimpses the spirits of relatives and friends who have already died, and a loving, warm spirit of a kind he has never encountered before – a being of light – appears before him. This being asks him a question, non-verbally, to make him evaluate his life and helps him along by showing him a panoramic, instantaneous playback of the major events in his life. At some point he finds himself approaching some sort of barrier or border, apparently representing the limit between earthly life and the next life. Yet he finds that he must go back to the earth, that the time for his death has not yet come. At this point he resists, for by now he is taken up with his experiences in the afterlife and does not want to return. He is overwhelmed by intense feelings of joy, love and peace. Despite his attitude, though, he somehow reunites with his physical body and lives.
>
> Later he tries to tell others, but he has trouble doing so. In the first place, he can find no human words adequate to describe these unearthly episodes. He also finds that others scoff, so he stops telling other people. Still, the experience affects his life profoundly, especially his views about death and its relationship to life.[9]

Because this is a constructed model, it lacks personal and experiential detail such as exists in a personal witness. It has to maintain a certain descriptive objectivity, but all such detail is supplied by a perusal of the many testimonies. There is much beauty and intuitive wisdom in some of the descriptions. The light which many describe is not blinding, but soft and radiant; there is a network of thought-communication, a heightened sense of perception, and feelings of peace, ease and quietness. There is often the later reflection that the fear of death is no more, and the joyful anticipation of meeting loved ones. The question of whether God exists does not arise in that form, but is rather beyond language, for as one woman said; 'I can't describe it, but the totality and reality of the living God exploded within my being and He filled every atom of my body with His glory.'

Before such research was presented publicly, there was reticence about sharing these experiences, but members of the medical profession themselves are coming to affirm survival after death as the basis of their research. Dr Raymond Moody says of himself: 'I have come to accept as a matter of religious faith that there is a life after death, and I believe that the phenomenon we have been examining is a manifestation of that life.'[10]

We are used to public declarations of faith by Christians who witness to the saving, forgiving power of Christ, echoed by the man born blind whose healing was discounted by unbelieving pharisees in St John's Gospel. They protested that Christ could not have healed him because he was a sinner, and the man retorts: 'Whether he is a sinner, I do not know; one thing I know, that though I was blind, now I see'.[11] There's no gainsaying that! In similar vein, one young man who was revived after apparent death reflects:

> It's funny. It's something that there is no way that it could possibly exist, and yet you know without a doubt that it does.
>
> Now I know that a lot of people will not believe this . . . People will come out and say that scientifically this cannot exist . . . But, you know what? It won't change a thing. Because just as sure as I'm sitting here now, if I died again today, virtually the same thing would happen, except that I could observe it better. And they can tell me it's not, and they can swear that it's not, and they can show me scientific evidence that it's not . . . and all I can do is say, 'Well, I know where I've been.'[12]

Sister death: friend, not enemy

I have not included the above paragraphs in the sense of marshalling evidence to convince anyone of human survival, for the Christian hope is not based upon such evidence or research. But it is foolish to ignore it, and it is certainly confirmatory to the believer who already affirms the loving care of God here, and beyond death's door. Also, it is not simply of survival that the Christian hope speaks, but of joy, of consummation and of a new plane of existence, a new dimension in which we shall have room to live and grow into the fulness of God, no longer hampered by finitude and mortality, but vibrant with resurrection life, in a new body of immortality.

Towards the end of St Francis' life, he was visited by a doctor from Arezzo, and Francis asked him a question:

> He asked him; 'What does thou think of my condition?'
>
> 'Brother,' replied the doctor with circumspection, 'I think that with the divine grace you will do well.'
>
> 'I pray thee not to hide the truth from me because I am indifferent whether I live or die. I am only desirous to accomplish the will of God.'
>
> 'In that case,' said the doctor, 'I must tell thee that according to our science, thy malady is incurable and in my opinion thou wilt die at the end of September or the beginning of October.'
>
> Raising his arms to heaven, the sick man joyfully cried: 'Be thou welcome, my sister Death.' Then turning to a friar he said: 'Call Brother Angelo and Brother Leo to come and sing beside my bed.'
>
> In spite of their tears, the two Brethren intoned the Canticle of the Sun; but this time before the final doxology, the sick man stopped them and added the following verse: 'Praised be my Lord for our Sister the Death of the Body from whom no man escapeth. Woe to him who dieth in mortal sin. Blessed are they who are found walking by Thy

most Holy Will, for the second death shall have no power to do them harm.'

Some, even among the brothers, were scandalised when they heard such singing and joy at the dying bed of St Francis, especially as he was in such a state of deterioration. Brother Elias remonstrated with him: 'Well-beloved Father,' he said, 'for my part I rejoice that thou shouldst be joyful; but this city which regards thee as a saint, I fear it will be scandalised to see that thou dost not prepare thyself for death in quite another manner.'

'Leave me, Brother,' replied Francis, 'for in spite of what I endure, I feel myself so near to God, that I cannot hold myself from singing.'

At the last, on Saturday, 3rd October, the brothers placed Francis on the ground in a coarse sack-cloth, covered his head with ashes and dust, and Psalm 142 was intoned with both sadness and strange joy. It was about an hour after sunset, and one of his biographers says: 'He died singing, in the forty-sixth year of his age and twenty-fifth of his conversion.' And another speaks of the radiance of his body:

> As for his body, it was, so to speak, transformed. For long contracted by suffering, his members had become supple like those of a child; his face was as beautiful as the face of an angel; the wound in his side seemed like a red rose; and on his flesh, but yesterday so husky, now a milky pallor shone; the Stigmata on his hands and his feet stood out like black pebbles on white marble. One would have said the Divine Crucified descended from His Cross.[13]

So death is no longer the enemy, but may become a friend. The 'real world' which we hear so much about becomes then no longer this arrogant, violent, grasping, materialistic world-system, but true life in God, beginning in this world, but continuing in its unfolding glory in the physical dissolution of the body. It will then be clearly experienced that it is not the physical body and the material world which is alone real (though of course it has its own precious reality when given to love). But it will be realised that all that is mortal and material must pass away, and the true individual identity will enter into the communion of saints, to participate in the triune life of God in fulness and vision and glory. This is not to reject the positive aspects of this life and of our world, but to see them in true perspective. As Martin Israel understands it:

> Our life on earth is an invitation to partake fully of the glory of the world. This glory consists, certainly, of the material riches of the earth, but there is something more in store for us. It is the discovery of the core of identity deep within us that survives the changes of the world outside us, and grows in stature, even when the material world falls from us at the moment of death. We are not fully alive until we can confirm, through the experience of our life, that inner core which is our proof of purpose, meaning, and destiny.[14]

Ministry to the dying

Sooner or later we have to face our own death, and rather than take heed to the popular song which says: 'Enjoy yourself – it's later than you think', it would be better for us to take heed to wiser words: 'Prepare yourself – it's later than you think'. The fact is that most of us have known children, young people and middle-aged, who have been diagnosed as terminally ill, with only months to live. Whether we have come to terms with such a diagnosis for ourselves or our relatives/friends, we need to know the possible pattern of experience which lies before us in such a case.

First of all there is the matter of sharing. I find it particularly sad that a man and wife, a father and daughter, a mother and son, feel obliged to hide from each other the fact that one of them is soon to die. Pretence, hypocrisy, subterfuge and play-acting are words which could be used if it were not done for the sake of love. It is not worthy of love, or of the loved one, that you should hide from him the fact that he is soon to die. A husband and wife who have shared all the happy, blissful days of falling in love, of youth spent together in physical, mental and spiritual union, and of a life and family with open secrets, with a mingling of joy and sorrow – such a couple should not be separated by the dark secret of suffering and death. Only as such a secret is shared can it be entered into, borne creatively, and bring forth new and profound depths of love which will carry first the one, and then the other, into the dimensions of eternity. The time between the home-call of one and the other will then be a time of precious memories, of a life lived together in all the joys and sorrows of ecstasies and pain.

I am not suggesting, of course, that a seemingly terminal diagnosis be communicated suddenly, or even professionally, without the context of preparation and loving relationship. Indeed it may be that no words need communicate it at all. What I am suggesting is that the truth be always told, though not *all* of it need be told at once, and that questions be always answered. For the depth at which the patient will question is the depth of his desire to know. He must be able to trust his loved ones, to know if things are all right, and to know if he must prepare for the journey into death. After all, he may have wrong relationships to put right, mistakes that need to be righted, letters that need to be written, gifts that need to be given, and a soul that needs to be saved. He may want to ask for holy communion, for sacramental anointing and the laying-on of hands. Making his confession, leading to holy communion shared with his loved one/s, may be the last joyful act of a life ready to be offered up in death. What a comment on our secular society are these words by Dr Maurice Rawlings:

> I remember one elderly patient who existed in a depressed atmosphere in a rather repugnant nursing home. A

forgotten patient among other deprived souls he was treated as a protoplasmic nonentity. One day he became acutely ill with pneumonia, was transferred to the nearest hospital where antibiotics, oxygen, and intravenous medications were to no avail. Although medical treatment was good, he died. He had received no treatment of the emotions and no care for the soul. He was friendless, frightened, forgotten, and alone. There was no opportunity for him to talk to anyone about finance, family, religion, or death. And no one asked him if he was prepared for life after death.[15]

Fortunately, it is not always like that. As I write, my own father is in a nursing home with frequent access of family, and where, last month, my frail and elderly mother and I were with him on his 82nd birthday, when matron and nursing staff carried in a birthday cake they had made, burning with candles. He is blind, and with emphysema, but he valiantly got enough breath to blow (most of) them out. 'Happy birthday' was sung to him, and a special birthday tea was distributed. And we prayed together in love and tears, within that week of being with him every day, in the midst of caring staff.

In the geriatric wing of a hospital in which I once worked in Swansea, there was a relationship between staff and patients which was often as full of hilarity and shared joy as of quietness and suffering. Both the sharing of joy and the alleviation of suffering were contained in the sustaining care which was given. And such care embraced both patients who had loved ones visiting them regularly, and patients who had relatives who never even bothered to enquire about them.

Even as I write, some of these patients parade before my imagination, and I greet them as old friends again. Dear old Frankie who was paralysed and had lost his speech in a single, massive stroke, could only lie in bed, or sit in his chair, but how many hours of non-verbal communication took place between us. He grumbled and laughed, indicated his frustration and his joy, his bad temper and his sense of humour in all manner of wordless ways. I say 'wordless', but Frankie did have an amazing capacity for song. He had the ability to maintain a tune with the syllables 'la-la-la', and in this way he not only called our attention to his needs with a monotoned 'la-la-la', but he sang for us. For instance:

> La-la-la-la-la; / la-la-la-la-la, Waltzing Matilda, Waltzing Matilda, La-la-la-la-la-la-la-la-la-la. You'll come a-waltzing, Matilda, with me . . .

and so on. Perhaps I remember him so clearly because on the day I left the hospital to return to theological training, I went to say goodbye to him. As I held his hand and talked with him, his 'la-la-la' language became subdued, and tears ran down his face. It would have been easier to have quietly slipped away, and sent him a letter, but we both needed to share the pain and joy of parting. Even now I commend him to the eternal love of God, in whose presence I am sure he is safe.

Stages in the process of dying

I'm writing on joy in life and death, and having known something of the sadness and joy of dying patients, I felt immense gratitude to read of the tremendous compassion and painstaking love exemplified by Dr Elisabeth Kübler-Ross in her work both with terminally ill patients and with medical and theological students. And if there is a book on this area that I would put into the hands of all 'theologs and medics' it would be her work, *On Death and Dying*. She outlines a five-fold pattern in the process from terminal diagnosis to dying, which emerges from interviews with more than two hundred patients, and this is the kind of pattern with which we should become acquainted in coming to terms with our own situation or that of a loved one.

1. *Denial*

This is a reaction sometimes of terror or fright. The denial is first of all within oneself, and then it may be a protestation to the medical staff. 'It can't be true – perhaps there has been a wrong diagnosis, a mix-up of patients – I want another opinion . . .' But there is a useful function served in such denial, as it acts as a kind of buffer so that the first 'numbing' enables the patient to come to terms with what may be horrific news. This stage does not happen to everyone. Some patients know intuitively that they are approaching death, and others may receive the news quietly, and need a time of solitude to digest it, or company to share it. With more technological and depersonalising equipment in intensive care units, there is all the more reason why patients should have access to loved ones when necessary, and that medical care does not impede personal relationships. It is better that a man dies *now*, surrounded by loved ones and prayer, than that he lives for another month or two surrounded by gadgets and 'life-saving'(!) equipment.

2. *Anger.*
This often follows the denial of the first terminal diagnosis. 'I am going to die' and there are feelings of resentment, jealousy and even rage. Blame is apportioned to relatives, friends, medical staff, and frequently to God. If staff and relatives understand that this is a 'phase' it is easier to face it, receive it, allow it to be, realising that it will give way to another phase, and eventually to a more balanced and accepting situation. If the patient should die suddenly in this phase, the relatives can then understand that the process had not gone its full course. And if there is a faith-dimension they can commend the loved one to God's love.

3. *Bargaining.*
This may be brief, and reveals itself in different ways. It includes good behaviour to placate God, or multiple promises of dedication of life or gifts of money 'if only God will spare my life'. Nominal Christians and nominal atheists are the ones who call upon God in this way at this stage. Christians and

atheists with a profounder and maturer understanding of life know that bargaining is not worthy of God (if he exists at all!).

4. *Depression.*
This is often the fourth stage in this pattern. When the extremely ill patient can no longer deny his condition, anger and rage give way to melancholy and loss. It is not just that medicine can do no more, surgery has failed and health has gone, but there is at last the realisation that I am mortal, and even that all hope is at an end. As I said above, profound Christians and atheists of integrity have more stability than people of nominal belief–lukewarm Christians. Such depression can take many forms – a breakdown of communication, a melancholy weariness and negativity, or a turning of the face to the wall to die.

5. *Acceptance.*
The fifth stage may be a positive facing of death with a certain equilibrium, or a mere resignation and withdrawl from life with a negative attitude that leads to a passivity in the face of death. There may be absence of 'feelings' now, and a diminishing of outside interests. Silence and non-verbal sharing may be what is needed. In the Christian experience (as in all the great faiths), this acceptance may reveal itself upon a graduated scale from quiet, tranquil acceptance, to joyful and yearning anticipation, with a positive underlying attitude which is basic to the experience of grace.

Of course, like all categorising, this process remains a general outline, a theoretical model, but it has been drawn from real experience of people in the situation of terminal illness, and it is part of the preparation process to be acquainted with such research and objective evaluation. If patients, family and friends understood this process, the sharing would become easier, the relationship more trusting, and the process of dying becomes one which would yield positive experience to all involved in that drama which is part of all our lives.

Often members of the family are uncomfortable and inadequate around the dying patient, and that is understandable in a society like ours which is unable to face the inevitable fact of death. One of the graves I dug while I was a garden-brother in our Dorset friary was for a brother who was remarkable for his childlikeness and simplicity. Some of us were embarrassed when he came on mission with us, because we never knew what he might say from the pulpit, and some of us thought ourselves more sophisticated in our knowledge of what was acceptable pulpit communication. He startled us in his beautiful simplicity not only in a mission sermon at Market Drayton, but also on another occasion which impinges on our present discussion.

A priest was just coming out of a hospital ward where a dying child was surrounded by his family – an occasion of great pain and helplessness, and the priest just felt inadequate to the situation. He met Brother N on the way out, and said something like: 'Oh, N, are you going in to see the child? I'm terribly sorry, but I was just unable to give any help.' So Brother N went in, and with a simplicity and gentleness he took the child's hand, prayed and spoke gently, and just spontaneously met the human and spiritual need out of the overflow of his own experience. It was not a studied attitude, a planned action or a mechanical approach. It emerged from who he was, from his loving and his simplicity – and, may I say, from his very naïveté. He manifested the grace of which Jesus spoke when he said: 'Unless you turn and become like children, you will never enter the kingdom of heaven.'[16]

Beyond all pain

This is the title of a small but moving collection of meditations for the suffering and bereaved, selected by Cicely Saunders, founder of the St Christopher's Hospice for the Dying, in 1967. Among the collection is a series of poems by Sidney Reeman, who had inoperable cancer of the gullet, and spent the last four months of his life at St Christopher's.

During that time he started writing poetry again after a long gap, and the eight poems included are both beautiful and painful to read. It is difficult to to know what to quote, but there are two which capture the experience of contained suffering and of joyful anticipation, right at the borderland of life and death. The first is called 'Coming up for the Third Time':

> Lord, in the last six days,
> I have felt peculiarly plaintive,
> Strength seems to be ebbing away,
> My tale is a tale of woe.
> Now in the midst of a melancholy moment
> Preoccupation about pain
> And thoughts squandered about swallowing
> I realise that I am
> A man of little faith,
> And it is certainly true
> That if Christ were to beckon me
> Across the waves, immediately
> I should begin to sink
> Through sheer lack of confidence.
> Lord, confirm me in faith
> Each time you come with comfort
> As the Bread of Life, then
> I shall realise that the Divine Strength
> Is not ebbing away,
> But gathering in intensity.

This sounds like a modern Gerontius, moving out of life into the mystery and wonder of death. The last of his poems was written just four days before his death, in which he writes of a lost two days, but also of the wonder of the last fortnight of being sustained in the hospice by the very bread and life of God. It is a worthy poem with which to conclude this chapter because it speaks of joy in life and death, and comes from the basic reality of a dying man entering into the divine mystery of God, beyond the gates of death.

Lost Property

Priceless is that which I have lost
Priceless because irretrievable.
Two days at least seemed
To have passed me by
In a fortnight of existence.
Rather uncanny
To think yesterday is today
And today is yesterday
But the hospice has given reassurance
As well as sustenance,
Has given me twelve large hampers
Duly strained and liquidised,
The Bread of Life here below,
The Great Supper is awaiting
Ever awaiting.

Sidney G. Reeman
24th February 1975

Sidney died in the morning of 1st March 1975.[17]

Notes

1 *English Hymnal*, 744.
2 *Wesley's Hymns* (1779), 49.
3 1 Corinthians 15:26.
4 Romans 8:18.
5 1 Corinthians 15:19.
6 Elisabeth Kübler-Ross, *On Death and Dying* (London: Tavistock Publications); Dr Raymond Moody, *Life After Life* (London: Corgi Books); *Reflections on Life After Life* (Illinois: Bantam Books); Drs Karlis Osis and Erlendur

Haraldsson, *At the Hour of Death* (New York: Avon Books).
7 Dr Maurice Rawlings, *Beyond Death's Door* (London: Sheldon Press).
8 For a contemporary British descriptive practice, see *First Aid Manual* (authorised by St John Ambulance, St Andrew's Ambulance Association and The British Red Cross Society) pp. 10–23.
9 Moody, *Reflections on Life After Life*, pp. 5f.
10 Ibid., p. 111
11 John 9:25.
12 Moody, *Reflections on Life After Life*, p. 111.
13 See Omer Englebert, *St Francis of Assisi* (London: Burns & Oates), pp. 299ff. There are some chronological difficulties in the life of St Francis. He is generally thought to have died in his 44th year.
14 Martin Israel, *Precarious Living* (London: Hodder & Stoughton), p. 11.
15 Rawlings, *op. cit.*, p. 124. See also the excellent chapter 'On the Fear of Death', in Kübler-Ross, *On Death and Dying*, pp. 1–8.
16 Matthew 12:3.
17 Cicely Saunders, *Beyond All Pain* (London: SPCK), pp. 61,63.

12 Joy in Crossing Over

There is no death

It is quite clear to the reader of this book that the author is committed. Not committed to a doctrine, creed or dogma, but to a Person – Jesus Christ. And with that person – Jesus incarnate, crucified and risen – he is carried into the mystery of God. The pattern of this mystery is triune, for it means that I have been moved and haunted by the breathing of God's Holy Spirit through creation ever since my childhood. At the age of twelve years I was summoned to the love and obedience of Christ, so that the shape of my human life has since been patterned on his, as delineated in the New Testament. And 'beyond' that dual pattern of Spirit and Son, the immense mystery of the divine Love has ever warmed me, seared me, caused me to tremble to the depths of my being.

I say these things at the beginning of this chapter because the task of writing it has caused me much heart-searching. The questions that arise for this and the next chapter, in my own heart, are those of content: What shall I say? How much shall I communicate? How do I differentiate between the revelation, my experience of it, and my interpretation of the experience? And of communication: How is it possible to share theological experience? *Ought* I to share at this level? How can I communicate *this* faith-experience without being misunderstood, giving a wrong impression or implying that experiential faith is an easy, trivial matter, begotten by a superficial understanding of the great mysteries of God, of life, of death?

I am continually aware that the affirmation of love in a world of suffering, of forgiveness in a world of hatred and of immortality in a world of disease, decay and death is no easy task. The circumstances of this chapter have brought me to write in the shadow of my father whom I visit frequently at home, and of one of our older friars, both of whose mortal condition deteriorates, as I write, towards physical dissolution, and who need constant nursing care by day and night.

But as I speak of the shadow of death, there is within me the constant affirmation of the eternal Love in whom the springs of light and joy break forth with renewed hope through the Gospel of life and immortality. I write today before an upstairs window of the monastery at Glasshampton on a clear, crisp December day. There is a beautiful chestnut tree before me in the field beyond the laurel hedge. It stands stark and bare under the grey winter sky, with the ragged remnants of crisp, dried leaves clinging here and there, its branches moving rhythmically in the gentle wind. And I know that it contains a great secret within its centre, and that unseen, the root-network reaches deep down into the profound mystery of humus and darkness below. I know that it will maintain its silent and naked witness throughout the coming months of frost, ice and cold. It will be shaken by the winds, soaked by the rains, and stand a sentinel in the falling snow. I've seen it before. But I also know that the secret of springtime is locked within its being, and that when the time is right the ground will soften, the year will turn, the warmth will come, the sun will shine. Then the sap will rise, unknown, unsuspected to the faithless eye, and the glory of resurrection will fulfil its yearly cycle and all the world will sing again. This is the pattern of the Gospel, reflected and re-enacted in my own human and spiritual life. When the Christian says 'There is no death', he is not denying the mortal reality of physical dissolution, or the pain and sadness of bereavement and earthly loss. And he certainly cannot deny the awful reality of the immoral labour and concentration camps in which thousands of human beings have been, and are, thrust to a premature and horrific death. But what he is affirming is the eternal dimension, the Love that knows no end, the Life that will not die. And what he is denying is that death has any *ultimate* power, any reality of its own, any rootedness in the eternal order in which the victory remains with Love. It is from this Gospel perspective that the apostle cried out with great gladness:

> Death is swallowed up in victory
> O death, where is thy victory?
> O death, where is thy sting?[1]

Of course, such an affirmation is of the nature of faith. It is not shared where the categories of scientific technology (good as they are in certain respects) are seen to be the ultimate criteria for human life and fulfilment. This materialistic standpoint is one of unfaith and is widespread in our secular, Western world. Neither is such affirmation shared where theology has been adulterated by secular materialistic philosophies, or reduced and emasculated so that supernatural and transcendent categories have been existentialised into mere symbols representing human worth or altruistic motivation. Human survival, immortality and resurrection are categories of faith, and only people of faith can affirm them. They not only impinge on present human existence, but saturate contemporary experience with hope in a hopeless world. The affirmation that man does not perish with the beasts also opens up the dimension of justice through judgment in the life to come, and gives the power not only to endure and survive in this world, but actually to 'take up arms' (albeit of a spiritual and non-violent nature) against worldly and demonic powers – and this will mean disobeying and confronting unjust worldly political systems of the left and the right in the garb of totalitarianism.

The borderland of death

There is no need for the contemporary Christian to

feel apologetic about such an affirmation of life in God beyond the grave. There is more, and not less, need for such faith to be affirmed and celebrated in a world where the human person is devalued, and human life made so cheap. We are of infinite value to God and our ultimate worth is measured by his creative and redeeming love. The whole of the last chapter was taken up in a consideration of the experience of the believer in the approach of death. Without denying the seriousness of death's meaning, it was possible to discern a more profound understanding of the experience than is possible for the non-believer, and with the understanding of faith comes hope and joy – even in the face of death. However sympathetic the loved one, the physician or the priest may be, they can only *accompany* the dying person into the area of the borderlands between life and death. Loving nursing care, the gentle ministry of affirming tenderness and prayers of faith and hope can accompany the dying man, but the actual journey has to be made alone – I mean apart from all human aids from this side of the grave. What help and strength comes from God directly and indirectly from the other side is another matter. We do not have either exact understanding or the language in which to clothe what we know and intuit by faith, but this chapter is an indication of the light we have received, mingled with the prayers and hope of the writer.

The Dream of Gerontius

The Bible is full of illuminative flashes of vision and exposition concerning the life of the world to come, the nature of the resurrection body and the symbolic description of heaven and hell[2], and the biblical teaching, symbols and analogies have found their way into the Church's teaching on life after death. Extra-biblical material has been imported into much of the music and poetry on the four last things of Advent, that is, death, judgement, heaven and hell, as an examination of the classic *The Divine Comedy* by Dante Aligieri reveals. The latter includes beautiful poetic and theological insight of the highest order in terms of *L'Inferno, Il Purgatorio* and *Il Paradiso*, but one needs a master of some theological acumen to guide one through such an eschatological, dramatic allegory.[3] A shorter, simpler and more biblical journey is the one portrayed by John Henry Newman in his *Dream of Gerontius*, and when wedded to the haunting music of Edward Elgar, it becomes a theological and devotional journey of immense wonder and joy. I have found great delight in giving an exposition of *The Dream* to brothers and sisters of our own and other Orders, in two sessions, followed by a contemplative listening to parts one and two of the work. For me, Elgar's music brought to life the poetry of Newman. Outside the Bible, if there is any piece of theological devotion which I would recommend as an instruction and preparation for death, it would be this double work by Newman and Elgar. It is not enough to attend a public performance, with text in hand, though if you have never done that, then a great wonder is in store for you. But you must go on and listen, and listen, prayerfully, devotionally, theologically until the words and the music saturate your soul. I shall be sharing it again during Holy Week this year with our novices and professed brothers, and shall produce an exposition for personal and group participation.

Each time I prepare to listen, I feel that strange yearning for the divine Love springing up within my heart. The preparation of body in a certain passivity and rest in God, and the lifting up of the mind and heart in simple openness, are prerequisites to the awareness of the presence of God in the poetry and the music. The opening bars of music usher the hearer into the presence of death, as Gerontius, in his weakness, feels his mortal life ebbing away. Death calls to him, not only in the physical symptoms he recognises, but also by a sense of innermost abandonment, 'this emptying out of each constituent /And natural force by which I come to be'. In the midst of such extremity he cries to God, as the priest and believers around his bed intercede for him, calling upon the Lord of mercy and all the company of heaven, as he draws near to the gates of death.

In the experience of Gerontius there is the group of intercessors encircling him on earth as he prepares to leave his mortal body, and as the poem unfolds, there is the awareness of the encircling great cloud of witnesses in heaven, who pray for and sustain him in that last and important journey he must make. He is not alone, and the doctrine of the communion of saints, on earth and in heaven, becomes precious and vital to him in these moments.

The priest and people now begin their intercessions with great power and authority. They do not plead for him on the basis of human pity or sympathy, though, of course, that dimension is certainly present, but on the basis of the divine grace, and the merits and work of Jesus crucified, dead, buried and risen. It is the enlisting of Jesus, the great Intercessor, Mediator and Saviour who is to the forefront here, and such powerful pleading, in the merits of Christ, cannot be refused:

> By Thy birth, and by Thy cross,
> Rescue him from endless loss;
> By Thy death and burial,
> Save him from a final fall;
> By Thy rising from the tomb,
> By Thy mounting up above,
> By the Spirit's gracious love
> Save him in the day of doom.

Firmly I believe and truly

There is no self-justification here, no trusting in his own works or merit, no self-congratulation at the hour of death. But there is a new strength, a new awareness, a new ability, contrasted with the opening helplessness and dissolution. He powerfully affirms the faith once and for all delivered to the saints, beginning with the few Latin words of the work:

Sanctus fortis, Sanctus Deus,
De profundis oro te,
Misere, Judex meus,
Parce mihi, Domine.

Holy, Mighty One, Holy God
Out of the depths I cry to you,
Have mercy upon me, my Judge,
Pity me, O Lord.

He then continues in what has now become a classic Christian confession, found in the hymn books of most churches: 'Firmly I believe and truly,/God is Three, and God is One'. The hymn is of such theological power that it sustains Gerontius in his confession and praise of the triune God of salvation, until at last he feels again bodily collapse, sensing the presence and fear of powers of darkness which would taunt him and pluck him from the hand of God, if that were possible.

But there are spiritual weapons against such powers, and the believers around his bed take up the whole armour of God to quench the fiery darts of the evil one. They begin a 'recital theology', calling upon the God who rescued the patriarchs of old and whose power can again sustain Gerontius in these moments of dying, and take him to the divine Love. This litany of intercession is beautiful to the ear, and a faith which can sustain a dying soul with such affirmation is wonderful indeed. This brings us to the very gate of death, and as Gerontius passes through, he commends his soul to God in the words of Psalm 31, re-echoed in the dying words of Jesus: 'Into Thy hands, O Lord, into Thy hands.'

As Gerontius, in his dying moments, confesses the triune God, trusting wholly in the name and merits of Christ, so now priest and believers, representing the Church on earth, commit the believers's soul to God, in the powerful words of the *Commendation:*

Go forth upon thy journey, Christian soul!
Go from this world! Go, in the name of God
The Omnipotent Father, Who created thee!
Go, in the name of Jesus Christ, our Lord,
Son of the living God, who bled for thee!
Go, in the name of the Holy Spirit,
Who hath been poured out on thee!
Go in the name of Angels and Archangels;
In the name of Thrones and Dominations;
In the name of Princedoms and Powers;
And in the name of Cherubim and Seraphim, go forth!
Go, in the name of Patriarchs and Prophets;
And of Apostles and Evangelists,
Of Martyrs and Confessors,
In the name of holy Monks and Hermits;
In the name of holy Virgins;
And all Saints of God,
Both men and women, go! Go on thy course!
And may thy place today be found in peace,
And may thy dwelling be the Holy Mount
  Of Sion – through the same, through Christ our Lord.

So ends the first part of the *Dream of Gerontius*. A whole theology of dying has been poured into the words and music of an hour or so, and the joy of the great acts of God in Christ, and in the believer's soul, have been celebrated in praise and prayer.

Crossing over

I believe that if the Church is to recover its vital sense of God in the mysteries of creation and redemption, it must participate both in the evangelical and catholic nature of the Gospel. As we have seen from the first part of the *Dream of Gerontius*, the departing soul is prepared and fortified for the journey of death into the nearer presence of God by the profession of a faith which casts itself wholly and entirely on the grace and mercy of God in Christ. And although the journey must be made alone, for we are born alone and must die alone, yet as the newborn child is tended by the hands of physician, midwife and/or loved ones, sustained and protected in the moments of its vulnerability and need, so the departing soul is surrounded on earth and in heaven by the communion of saints.

Thus, in preparation for death, in the commendation of the departing soul, and in the eucharistic celebration of Jesus' risen life for the departed, there are the Catholic liturgical acts of love and prayer which we offer to our Lord for the loved one.

When there is the crisis of a sudden death, the Lord undertakes, for he is not tied to acts of ritual, prayer or sacrament. He is sovereignly free, and we can trust his grace to make up to the believer that which is lacking. But it is a great grace to have time to prepare for death.

Since I have been increasingly aware of the possibility that I shall spend a prolonged period in solitude and prayer, I have thought of the distinct possibility of dying alone, without help, without sacraments. Of course, none of us knows how or when we shall die, but as I reflect upon my own death, it makes more poignant and real the prayer which we pray at our service of benediction every Thursday at the monastery, called the *Anima Christi*:

> Soul of Christ, sanctify me,
> Body of Christ, save me,
> Blood of Christ, inebriate me,
> Water from the side of Christ,
>   wash me.
>
> Passion of Christ, strengthen me,
> O good Jesu, hear me,
> Within Thy wounds hide me,
> Suffer me not to be separated from Thee,
> From the malicious enemy defend me,

In the hour of my death call me,
And bid me come to Thee,
That with Thy Saints, I may praise Thee
For ever and ever. Amen.

But if we do have time to repent, time to prepare, time to reflect, there is the possibility of making one's confession to God, of being anointed before death, and of receiving holy communion as the medicine of immortality. Also, when loved ones are feeling their own helplessness in the face of death, it is encouraging to be able to participate in these simple acts of faith and love for the dying person. When I was a curate at St Mary's Episcopal Cathedral, Glasgow, the telephone rang one day, and the wife of a dying man whom I had visited the previous day told me that her husband was now very near to death. I got on my motor-cycle and within fifteen minutes was at the bedside, and there was such joy in saying the *Commendation* for the departing soul: 'Go forth upon thy journey, Christian soul . . .' during which the man quietly breathed his last.

I have never been able to understand the objection to prayers for the departed, for although I inherited such obection in my own early Protestant theology, one day I had sudden news of the suicide of a friend who had a psychiatric illness, and I found myself naturally praying for him, and commending him to the loving mercy of the Lord. And so it has always been since that time. It would be a very sad thing for a minister of God to go to the bedside of a person who has just died, and feel that there was nothing to be done, no prayers to be offered, no commending of the departed soul to the immense mercy of the God to whom death does not mean what it does to us. From our side there is a sad separation, the body in which life is extinct, a voice now fallen silent, and the mortal life taken away. But to God all are alive, and he is the Lord of life and death. To be able to minister to the departing soul is a very precious thing, for there are times when such a person will want to be led in the prayer of forgiveness and reconciliation, or the believer want you to accompany him to the very borders of the river of death. There is a lovely account of Hopeful's ministry to Christian as they come to that river in Bunyan's *Pilgrim's Progress*:

> They then addressed themselves to the water, and entering, Christian began to sink, and, crying out to his good friend Hopeful, he said, I sink in deep waters; the billows go over my head, all His waves go over me. Selah.
>
> Then said the other, Be of good cheer, my brother: I feel the bottom, and it is good. Then said Christian, Ah! my friend, the sorrows of death hath compassed me about, I shall not see the land that flows with milk and honey. And with that a great darkness and horror fell upon Christian, so that he could not see before him. Also here he in great measure lost his senses, so that he could neither remember nor orderly talk of any of those sweet refreshments that he had met with in the way of his pilgrimage.
>
> (But Hopeful said), These troubles and distresses that you go through in these waters, are no sign that God hath forsaken you; but are sent to try you, whether you will call to mind that which heretofore you have received of His goodness, and live upon Him in your distresses.
>
> Then I saw him in my dream, that Christian was in a muse awhile. To whom also Hopeful added these words, Be of good cheer, Jesus Christ maketh thee whole. And with that Christian brake out with a loud voice, Oh, I see Him again; and He tells me, When thou passest through the waters, I will be with thee; and through the rivers, they shall not overflow thee.
>
> Then they both took courage, and the enemy was after that as still as a stone, until they were gone over. Christian therefore presently found ground to stand upon, and so it followed that the rest of the river was but shallow. Thus they got over.[4]

The time between

From the moment of the believer's death until the *parousia*, the coming again of Christ in glory at the last day, there is a time between. Some Christians have thought of this time as 'soul sleep'. I was quite fascinated in my early evangelical days by meeting, at a powerful evangelistic mission, one of the evangelists for the *Society for Evangelising London*, who believed in soul sleep and the final annihilation of the impenitent. It ran counter to the teaching which I had received, that the departed soul's destiny was fixed for heaven or hell, and that hell was a place (or perhaps a state) of quasi-physical, conscious torment of eternal duration. It was not long before doubts crept in about such a doctrine, because I had come to know the God and Father of our Lord Jesus Christ, and the amazing extent of his redeeming love. So when again I heard the preaching of a saintly man in a fervent fundamentalist context, and discovered again that *he* did not believe in the doctrine of everlasting conscious punishment of the wicked, I decided to ask questions. One of the joyful answers I got about this man was that the pulpit was not closed to him (in spite of his heretical opinions!) because his life was so saintly and his preaching so loving. What a recommendation! I did wonder if he was more saintly than God – if the doctrine I was taught was true!

I was never attracted to the doctrine of 'soul sleep' anyway, but was perplexed about the state of a partially sanctified believer. At the moment of death was he suddenly immortalised, perfected, and did he enter into the complete and final and absolute vision of the dazzling mystery of God? It was too much!

It was clear to me then, as it is now, that a doctrine of purgatory which involved suffering for or paying for one's sins, with the added notion of monetary payment and the purchase of indulgences to free souls from purgatory's pains, was against the spirit and letter of the Gospel, as well as against common sense. Such a doctrine easily paved the way for a necessary reformation. I saw the point of Luther's protest against

Tetzel's hawking around of indulgences for sale, with the placard which indicated;

> As soon as the coin in the coffer rings
> The soul from purgatory springs . . .[5]

And it was no use to say that this was an adulteration of the Church's doctrine, for that was how the people understood and received it. And yet it also seemed to me that if the process of sanctification was to make the redeemed sinner more worthy of the divine presence, then that process had to be seen in its fulness, as a work of the Holy Spirit within the believer, and I saw no reason why that should cease at death. For if the soul was made instantly perfect, I wondered if such a creature would be the same person. It was clear that only One could, by suffering, merit or self-sacrifice, 'pay the price of sin'. That was Christ. There was to be no *post-mortem* redemptive suffering for sin. But the work of sanctification would surely continue, as the understanding of the 'nearer presence' of God was one which seemed to accommodate the gospel facts, and yet give room for what was more of a 'sanctificatory' than a purgatory! I do not mean that there would be no suffering – but that it would not be penal, a suffering of retribution or payment, but rather the kind of suffering that the believer knows in this life as the Holy Spirit sears and burns him in the crucible of the divine Love. It is significant that St Paul's *Judgment Seat of Christ* is for believers only, and involves a testing by fire![6] The sanctifying suffering to which I refer is that suffering *with* Christ, being crucified with him as we are conformed to his image. The remarkable thing is that this is what many Roman Catholic friends believe under the heading of *purgatory* anyway! They are far too gospel-centred to believe or preach Tetzel's propositions.

This brings us back to the *Dream of Gerontius*, as we remember that it was written by John Henry Newman who had been an Anglican, and he saw the drama of the journeying soul in just this kind of light. The second part of Elgar's setting opens with Gerontius waking from the sleep of death. The opening lines are poetry of a high quality, and worth quoting:

> I went to sleep; and now I am refreshed.
> A strange refreshment: for I feel in me
> An inexpressive lightness, and a sense
> Of freedom, as I were at length myself,
> And ne'er had been before. How still it is!
> I hear no more the busy beat of time,
> No, nor my fluttering breath, nor struggling pulse;
> Nor does one moment differ from the next.

He is now in the 'intermediate state', having left the body, but still on his journey. (Spatial and temporal terms are, of course, only analogies – for how else can we speak of the eternal dimension?) He 'feels' now the silence, solitude and profound rest, mixed with a loving sternness. He also feels himself to be held with a gentle pressure – not self-moving, but borne forward on the way. And then (touching his very heart) he hears the melody of love – the singing of his guardian angel and he/she (there is no angelic gender) sings to God in praise of the task which has been given to such a ministering spirit, to guide the heir of salvation into the nearer presence of God. This is the angel which has always ministered to Gerontius, without his knowledge, on earth, and now sings of the salvation which Gerontius has received as a gift of grace.

The ministry of angels is one which is clearly rooted in scripture, and to reflect upon it in the light of Newman's text in such an appropriate setting provided by Elgar, is to evoke gratitude and adoration before God. There is communication between earth and heaven within the work of God's salvation, and so the guardian angel sings:

My work is done,
  My task is o'er
    And so I come,
    Taking it home,
For the crown is won,
    Alleluia,
  For evermore.

My Father gave
  In charge to me
    This child of earth
    E'en from its birth,
To serve and save,
    Alleluia,
  And saved is he.

This child of clay
  To me was given,
    To rear and train
    By sorrow and pain
In the narrow way,
    Alleluia,
  From earth to heaven.

These are all 'moments' in the continuing work of sanctification. Gerontius is done with sin and punishment. He is a saved soul – but much sanctifying work has still to be done in him before he can gaze upon something of the loveliness of the incomprehensible God whom no man has seen or can see, who dwells in light unapproachable, and who only has immortality.[7] Gerontius recognises the angelic being as 'Mighty One, my Lord, my Guardian Spirit, all hail!' And the angel replies: 'My child and brother, hail!' So is effected a wondrous relationship in God between human soul and divine being, as Gerontius asks, not for information or 'speaking for speaking's sake', but for 'conscious communion', though there are things he would learn if it were not mere curiosity on his part. The angel assures him: 'You cannot now cherish a wish which ought not to be wished.' He is in a state of perpetual grace – this is what was accomplished in laying off his mortal flesh. There was a cleansing, a renewal, an infusion of new life effected, by which he is now no longer a sinner, but a cleansed, redeemed soul, approaching the blinding vision of the glorious God.

Gerontius then asks the question which has arisen in our minds, saying that he thought that at the very moment that the struggling soul quitted its mortal body, it immediately fell under the awful presence of God, therewith to be judged and sent to its own place. And he wants to know why he is hindered in such a course. The angel replies that there is no hindrance, but that he *is* hurrying with extremest speed to the threshold of heaven.

This stimulates further questioning. Gerontius wonders why he has no fear of meeting God, because during his life, the thought of death and judgment was terrible to him. And the reply comes (and this is mind-blowing theology) that because Gerontius *did* fear, now there is no fear; because he *did* submit to judgment, judgment for sin is now done:

> It is because
> Then thou didst fear, that now thou dost not fear.
> Thou has forestalled the agony, and so
> For thee bitterness of death is passed.
> Also, because already in thy soul
> The judgment is begun.

At this point there is an exposure to dark and demonic powers who desire to snatch unprepared souls, and although Gerontius listens to the sour and uncouth dissonance of their wailing, their envy and jealousy of redeemed souls, and the 'restless panting of their being' like beasts of prey, he is no longer afraid of the hungry and wild spirits that taunt and shriek. And as the cacophony of their cries fades into the distance, he asks another question; 'Shall I see my dearest Master, when I reach His throne?' And the angel answers from a depth of wisdom, that he does not know what he asks – he *shall* see, but that sight will both gladden and pierce the very depths of his soul. And Gerontius suddenly feels an awe fall upon him, and a fearful wonder.

I remember the first time I understood the words which follow. In one stanza I was filled and enamoured with trembling and love. It is the angel's answer that one mortal did gaze upon the unutterable glory of the crucified Christ, and received in his own body the marks of the stigmata – St Francis of Assisi:

> There was a mortal, who is now above
> In the mid glory: he, when near to die
> Was given communion with the Crucified –
> Such, that the Master's very wounds were stamped
> Upon his flesh; and, from the agony
> Which thrilled through body and soul in that embrace,
> Learn that the flame of the Everlasting Love
> Doth burn ere it transform.

The ministry of sanctification continues in Gerontius' soul by words such as these, for as the journey progresses, so does the work of interior transformation. He is knowing a deeper *purgation*, a profounder *illumination*, leading to *union* with God in love that will transform the very structures of his being. So having passed through the gate, and within the house of Judgment, Gerontius hears the choir of angelicals who sing the words which we have come to know: 'Praise to the Holiest in the height . . .' This becomes a hymn of adoration, setting forth the great themes of the Gospel – the redemption of Adam's race by the Second Adam, sung by choirs of angelicals, to the glory and adoration of God.

The veiled presence of God

When I speak of the 'intermediate state' and indicate a time sequence in the soul's sanctification, I am endeavouring to speak of an existence on the other side of death which is not subject to the spatial and temporal laws that we know in the body. In this sense, the descriptions of a process which are before us in the *Dream of Gerontius* are not to be understood as chronologically progressive, for time is no more in that dimension. Nevertheless, Gerontius is being progressively 'prepared' for that momentary gaze upon the Being of God, the sight of Whom will smite him, pierce him, burn and sear him with its holiness and blazing love. 'The judgment now is near,' says the angel, 'for we are come into the veiled presence of our God.' Gerontius hears the voices he left on earth still praying around his bed, and then he beholds a great wonder, the Angel of the Agony, who alone could strengthen Christ in the hour of his Gethsemane suffering:

> Before the Throne
> Stands the great Angel of the Agony,
> The same who strengthened Him, what time He knelt
> Lone in the garden shade, bedewed with blood.
> That Angel best can plead with Him for all
> Tormented souls, the dying and the dead.

In contrast to the tender and loving voice of the guardian angel, here is an angel of great might and power. The reverberations of the agony of Gethsemane are heard in his voice as he pleads before the Throne, intercedes with the great Intercessor, and pleads the passion of Christ for Gerontius, and for all those who have died in the body, and wait with patience and longing to gaze upon their glorious Lord, like the souls under the altar in the Apocalypse.[8] The theme of such powerful intercession is taken up by the angelicals and then by the guardian angel, who is well aware of the 'aweful glance' of God that will soon smite Gerontius beyond anything he has ever known in life on earth or in the heavenly places. The intercession continues:

> Praise to His Name!
> O happy, suffering soul! for it is safe,
> Consumed, yet quickened by the glance of God.
> Alleluia! Praise to His Name!

Then begins the ascending crescendo of anticipation, which moves towards a terrible climax as the veil is slowly drawn aside and Gerontius gazes upon the ineffable vision, the dazzling mystery of the incomprehensible Godhead, which reaches the moment of climax and of dazzling glory – which strikes, and wounds – and Gerontius cries out in agony of longing, 'Take me away . . .' *In this moment* he has realised as never before his total unworthiness, his finitude, the chasm of creatureliness which causes him to cover his eyes, and to cry from the lowest depths. It is a moment of supreme pain and supreme joy. But now he knows! Now he is aware of all the implications of all his questions, and he feels the sorrow and the joy which penetrate his being, for he longs for God.

This 'time between', this 'intermediate state', is what I used to call 'sanctificatory', for it is not a place but a mode of being, and a way of being embraced by the beauty, wonder, and purifying fire of God's love. If 'purgatory' had not such a bad history, and was shorn of all its unbiblical abuses, it could have been used to indicate that process of anticipation and of the continuing sanctifying work of the Holy Spirit. Certainly in *The Dream of Gerontius* the souls in purgatory are singing Psalm 90, as the angel sings the song of tender farewell until the morrow of the great day, the coming again of Christ in glory:

> Farewell, but not for ever! brother dear,
> Be brave and patient on thy bed of sorrow;
> Swiftly shall pass thy night of trial here,
> And I will come and wake thee on the morrow . . .

The Pilgrim's Progress

We don't have to take the text of *Gerontius* as other than an *interpretation* of the soul's progress from earth to heaven, though I have found that the contemplative listening to the poem set to Elgar's glorious music is most satisfying theologically as well as devotionally. But in the Bunyan tradition, there is also this matter of an intermediate state, and the ministry of angels, which is succinctly stated after Christian and Hopeful have come through the river of death, and landed on the other side:

> Now upon the bank of the river, on the other side, they saw the two shining men again, who there waited for them. Wherefore being come out of the river, they saluted them, saying, We are ministering spirits, sent forth to minister for those that shall be heirs of salvation. Thus they went along towards the gate.
>
> Now you must note, that the City stood upon a mighty hill; but the pilgrims went up that hill with ease, because they had these two men to lead them up by the arms: also they had left their mortal garments behind them in the river; for though they went in with them, they came out without them. They therefore went up here with much agility and speed, though the foundation upon which the City was framed was higher than the clouds; they therefore went up through the regions of the air, sweetly talking as they went, being comforted because they safely got over the river, and had such glorious companions to attend them.
>
> The talk that they had with the shining ones was about the glory of the place; who told them that the beauty and glory of it was inexpressible. There, said they, is the Mount Sion, the heavenly Jerusalem, the innumerable company of angels, and the spirits of just men made perfect. You are going now, said they, to the paradise of God, wherein you shall see the tree of life, and eat of the never-fading fruits thereof: and when you come there you shall have white

robes given you, and your walk and talk shall be every day with the King, even all the days of eternity. There you shall not see again such things as you saw when you were in the lower region upon the earth: to wit, sorrow, sickness, affliction and death; For the former things are passed away. The men then asked, What must we do in the holy place? To whom it was answered, You must there receive the comfort of all your toil, and have joy for all your sorrow; you must reap what you have sown, even the fruit of all your prayers, and tears, and sufferings for the King by the way. In that place you must wear crowns of gold, and enjoy the perpetual sight and visions of the Holy One; for there you shall see Him as He is. There also you shall serve Him continually with praise, with shouting and thanksgiving . . .[9]

Thus however the Christian understands the intermediate state between death and final consummation – there is freedom from the burden and pain of finitude and mortality. There is freedom from the nature of sin that plagues us during our earthly pilgrimage. And there is, above all, the increasing awareness of fellowship and loving union with Christ, being made more and more into his image, and anticipating the vision, glory and transfiguration of union in the mystery of God. St Paul was joyful in Christ, even in his prison cell, believing it to be part of his ministry and witness, but his yearning indicates the anticipated joy that welled up in his heart:

Christ will be honoured in my body, whether by life or by death. For to me to live is Christ, and to die is gain. If it is to be life in the flesh, that means fruitful labour for me. Yet which I shall choose I cannot tell. I am hard pressed betwen the two. My desire is to depart and be with Christ, for that is far better. But to remain in the flesh is more needful on your account.[10]

Notes

1 1 Corinthians 15:54f.

2 See 1 Corinthians 15; 2 Thessalonians 4:13–18; Revelation, *passim*.

3 Such a master is Dorothy L. Sayers in the translation and exposition she accomplished in *Dante: The Divine Comedy* (Harmondsworth: Penguin Books), 3 vols.

4 John Bunyan, *The Pilgrim's Progress* (London: Dent), pp. 156f.

5 Roland Bainton, *Here I Stand* (London: Mentnor), p. 9.

6 1 Corinthians 3:11–15.

7 1 Timothy 6:16.

8 Revelation 6:9f.

9 Bunyan, op. cit., pp. 157f.

10 Philippians 1:20–24.

13 Judgment and Eternal Joy

Compatibility of judgment and Love

Having written so much about the intermediate state, something must be said about judgment and hell. It is clear that scripture must be understood as compatible with itself, and with the character of God revealed to us in the saving Gospel of Christ. I have clearly stated that heaven is not a reward, but a gift of grace. It is the state of soul of the redeemed sinner in this life – 'where Jesus is, 'tis heaven there' – and in the life to come.

So hell is not punishment in an arbitrary sense of revenge or penal action – especially as conceived as eternal torment of the soul without hope or grace. John Macquarrie puts it like this: 'Hell is not some external or arbitrary punishment that gets assigned for sin, but is simply the working out of sin itself, as it destroys the distinctively personal being of the sinner.' And though he is careful in his qualifications, he goes on:

> This uttermost limit of hell would be annihilation, or at least the annihilation of the possibility for personal being. Since salvation is itself personal and must therefore be freely accepted, God cannot impose it upon anyone, so we must at least leave open the possibility that this kind of annihilation might be the final destiny for some.

Macquarrie is a biblical theologian with a keen sense of the authority of scripture, and it is therefore significant when he says of eternal punishment:

Needless to say, we utterly reject the idea of a hell where God everlastingly punishes the wicked, without hope of deliverance. Even earthly penologists are more enlightened nowadays. Rather we must believe that God will never cease from his quest for universal reconciliation, and we can firmly hope for his victory in this quest, though recognising that this victory can only come when at last there is the free cooperation of every responsible creature.[1]

John Hick comes from an early evangelical background, and this is reflected in his classic work *Evil and the God of Love*, which is a theology of theodicy (the reconciliation of the goodness, wisdom and power of God with the contrary evidence of evil, thereby 'justifying the ways of God to men'). But of the doctrine of everlasting torment in hell, he writes:

The sufferings of the damned in hell, since they are interminable, can never lead to any constructive end beyond themselves and are thus the very type of ultimately wasted and pointless anguish. Indeed misery which is eternal and therefore infinite would constitute the largest part of the problem of evil. Further, the notion of hell is no less fatal to theodicy if, instead of stressing the sufferings of the damned, we stress the fact that they are unendingly in sin. For this is presumably an even greater evil – a greater frustration of the divine purpose – than their misery. Thus in a universe that permanently contained sin, good and evil would be co-ordinates, and God's creation would be perpetually shadowed and spoiled by evil; and this would be incompatible either with God's sovereignty or with His perfect goodness. For the doctrine of hell has as its implied premise either that God does not desire to save all His human creatures, in which case He is only limitedly good, or that His purpose has finally failed in the case of some – and indeed, according to the theological tradition, most – of them, in which case He is only limitedly sovereign. I therefore believe

> that the needs of Christian theodicy compel us to repudiate the idea of eternal punishment.[2]

Hick states here the theological problem posed by the eternal existence of conscious human torment, and the continuity of rebellion against the divine Love. These were problems which faced me as a young Christian, and it was the Gospel itself, Jesus himself, the Bible itself, working through my enlightened Christian conscience, which caused me to reject, first of all, the doctrine of everlasting punishment as alien to the nature of God's love, and the doctrine of everlasting impenitence as alien to the nature of God's justice.

On a return visit, some time ago, to one of the churches in which I held pastoral charge, I was engaged in one of our theological/devotional talks with one of the members. She is a woman of spiritual discernment, and turning to me suddenly, she said, 'You don't believe in hell, do you?' smiling gently as she spoke.

'Now why do you ask that?' I queried.

'Well, I don't think I've ever heard you preach on hell.'

'But oh, I do,' said I, 'and you've often heard me preach on the justice of God's judgment.'

'But you know what I mean,' she insisted.

'Yes, of course I know what you mean. And the answer is no! I don't believe that God everlastingly punishes his human creatures in physical or spiritual torment without hope, without appeal, without end, in some kind of retribution which has no purpose of amendment or return in it.' She smiled again, nodding her head, and gave me a wise and knowing answer in which we shared—and we both felt something of the fear and awe of the Lord.

Three diverse theories

It would be sentimental and unreal, in order to speak of joy, to evade, deny or explain away the element of judgment. Indeed, judgment is part of joy, for the purpose of judgment is at least fairness and justice, and in the Christian faith based on holy scripture, God's judgment breaks forth into joyful justice, forgiveness, reconciliation. Therefore we must try to understand the warnings and judgments, interpreting them aright.

When scripture speaks of judgment for sin and for the finally impenitent, it is affirming something which we all feel to be the expression of our moral being. However symbolically we may interpret the 'Great White Throne' of the Apocalypse[3], there is certainly discrimination in the sense that good and evil are rewarded. The moral sense that differentiates between John the Baptist and Herod, Gandhi and Hitler, Martin Luther King and Stalin, is sound. Whether the separation is that of a 'moment' or a 'process' is a matter for reflection, but the fact of separation to judgment is clear, both in scripture and conscience. The principle and basis of that judgment is *character*, and in terms of the 'sheep and goats' judgment[4], that principle means likeness or unlikeness to the nature of Christ. And it is not that we are 'sent' to such judgment, but that we continue to follow our own direction. If our faces are towards the light, we shall be drawn more and more into its radiance, but if our faces are towards darkness, it will exercise its awful fascination over us. Ian MacLaren once said that it is as if sheep and swine are feeding together in a field. When night comes the sheep move towards the fold of their own accord, but the swine to the sty. It is their own choice. Each day we make our choices, and they have either to do with love and light or with evil and darkness – thus do we move towards judgment. In *The Great Divorce*, C. S. Lewis has a chilling statement: 'There are two kinds of people in the world: those who say to God, "Thy will be done," and those to whom God says, in the end, "Thy will be done."'

There is a certain reticence in the Bible, not about the *fact* of judgment, but about its *nature* and *duration*. But people have not been content to let the Judge of the earth do right in his own way, but have endeavoured to make doctrines out of texts, and theologies out of words. Proof-text theologies are often dangerous. It is far sounder to take a wider, panoramic view of the general teaching and progressive understanding included in the wide spectrum of scripture. There are three general theories which Christians hold to a greater or lesser degree, all of which have certain scriptural evidence, but all of which are partial and ultimately unsatisfactory as they are stated because of their conflict with other evidence. They are:

1. The theory of Everlasting Torment;
2. The theory of Conditional Immortality and Annihilation;
3. The theory of Universal Restoration.[5]

It is strange that three such conflicting theories could be deduced from the same Bible, but a partial consideration of the evidence, and the power of prejudice and preconceptions in estimating it, make it easier to see how such a thing can happen. Certainly the Bible maintains that it will be gloriously well with the good and unutterably evil with the wicked. There is clearly enunciated the sovereignty of the divine Love, and the malignity of sin and evil. And the matter of human freedom must be respected. But there is, throughout the Bible, a prophetic thread of promise which cannot envisage the victory of evil, sin and death forever. Ultimately, God's love and mercy will triumph, and evil shall not be eternal. This is not envisaged in this age, but in the age or ages to come, and it is well stated in the midway point of the Old and New Testaments in the early preaching of St Peter:

> This is how God fulfilled what he had foretold in the utterances of all the prophets: that his Messiah should suffer. Repent then and turn to God, so that your sins may be wiped out. Then the Lord may grant you a time of recovery and send you the Messiah he has already appointed, that is, Jesus. He must be received into heaven until the time of universal restoration comes (lit. the times

of the restoration of all things), of which God spoke by his holy prophets.[6]

The word *restoration* here, *apocatastasis*, is the word used by some of the early Eastern Fathers in their teaching on the reconciliation of all things, and it is found in its healing and restorative sense in different parts of the New Testament.[7]

With this in mind, we shall look at the three theories as they represent three different kinds of understanding within the Christian Church across the denominational board.

1. The theory of *Everlasting Torment* holds that the finally impenitent will be consigned to a hell of everlasting punishment and misery, with no reprieve and without correction, chastistement or hope. Some limit such a judgment to those who knowingly and consciously in this life reject Christ, but others include all who have not actually 'received' him in a conscious and personal manner.

It is increasingly clear that Christians of both Evangelical and Catholic traditions, while maintaining the basic element of moral judgment in the gospels, can no longer uphold a doctrine which envisages God as an omnipotent judge who sovereignly and willingly tortures creatures of his own making with everlasting misery, with no hope of escape or possibility of repentance, because their judgment has been fixed at death.

Only those who have been brought up, as I was, under such teaching, can believe that many good and charitable people believe such a thing. In my own experience, I constantly come across fellow-Christians who feel they must give lip-service to this party-line doctrine, and they hardly dare think about it, let alone discuss it. Again, I meet others who, because of such teaching in their earlier days, have jettisoned the whole Faith, because they feel that a Faith that teaches that God is such a tyrant and monster, is unworthy to appeal to ordinary human beings with basic charity and common sense, And there are others – I had a letter from one yesterday, and she has lived in constant fear and psychological torment because, although her mind tells her that such a thing cannot be (and she is an intelligent married woman), she cannot on an emotional level believe either that God is loving, or that she is accepted by him.

Alan Jones, in a remarkable new book on spirituality and theology, speaks of those who even have a 'particular affection' for the doctrine of everlasting punishment because it is thought to be a way of safeguarding the justice of God. He has this to say;

> I take the issue of moral choice very seriously, and believe that we suffer the consequences of our decisions. Our choices are critical, but I find no grounds for believing that the process of our making choices and living them through is irrevocably settled at death. God is just and life is sometimes 'hell'; but to insist as many do, that a person is damned *everlastingly* if he or she fails to make a personal and verbal commitment to Jesus Christ is both absurd and morally repellant. What about all those who haven't made a decision for Jesus Christ because of the terrible example of those who have? Are we believers not implicated in their damnation? I wonder sometimes how many people need to be in hell in order to make some 'Christians' feel safe?[8]

It is not just a matter of a just judgment, for God *does* hold the sinner accountable, and the *fact* of judgment is sure. But God's judgment is just, and contains elements of correction, leading to repentance. This doctrine not only teaches that God does not grant repentance because of a man's fixed state at death, but also that he keeps them alive and conscious to suffer for ever and ever. They must continue in their rebellion, impenitence and rejection of good, for they are not allowed repentance, and therefore there is co-existence of good and evil everlastingly. This is what the contemporary

Christian cannot maintain, and once it has been clearly stated and thought through, once the sovereignty of the divine Love has been affirmed in mind and heart, there is no going back. J. Paterson Smyth puts it like this:

> However fully Conscience recognises the righteousness of a terrible retribution for sin, there is in all thoughtful minds a shrinking from the thought that evil shall be as permanent as good in the universe of the All-holy God – that any evil power can exist unendingly side by side with Him and unendingly resist Him – that Hell and Heaven, Satan and God, shall co-exist for all eternity. This is almost unthinkable to thoughtful men. It is a dualism repugnant to all our ideals of God.[9]

One must be careful to avoid a superficial optimism about the nature of evil or the exceeding sinfulness of sin, but it cannot be, as some Christians seem to hold, that God is bound to carry out a sentence as judge, which he would forbear to do as Father. This is a strange kind of sophistry, for God is one. That memorable army chaplain G. A. Studdert Kennedy experienced an immense amount of suffering and pain in his ministry, and his understanding of the nature of God reflects the redeeming and reconciling Gospel in a poem he calls 'Eternal Hope':

> Can the Father in His Justice burn in everlasting flame
> Souls that, sunk in foulest squalor, never knew the Father's Name?
> Can the Love of man be greater than Eternal Love divine?
> Can the heart of God be harder than this hardened heart of mine?
> Can the pangs of Hell be endless, void of object, void of gain,
> Save to pay for years of sorrow with Eternity of Pain?

Cursèd be the foul contortion, that hath turned His Love to Hate,
That hath cried at death's dim portal, 'Enter here, and 'tis too late.'
Cruel pride and vain presumption claim to grasp where angels grope;
'Tis not God but mean man's blindness dims the deathless star of Hope.[10]

But even as I write these words, I can hear texts which are quoted to me to uphold such teaching, like, 'he that believeth not shall be damned,' 'how shall ye escape the damnation of hell', and 'these shall go away into everlasting punishment'. I cannot ignore texts like these, and at least the following comments must be made.

First, the word *damnation* has taken on a much darker meaning since the days of the King James Version of the Bible, and *condemnation* has taken its place as a more correct reading in the new versions – and I have no wish to deny that condemnation is due to sin and impenitence. The New Testament word is *katakrino*, and the correct translation is 'to judge adversely or condemn'. The earlier meaning I just referred to is illustrated in the Wycliffe Bible in the story of the woman caught in adultery. Jesus says; 'Woman, hath no man damned thee?' 'No man, Lord.' 'Neither do I damn thee.'

Then the word 'hell' appears eighteen times in the King James Version (A.V.) Once from the Greek *Tartaros*, which is a place/state of waiting; five times from the Greek *Hades* which again is a temporal place/state. The other twelve times it is a translation of *Gehenna*, which does not *itself* carry the idea of endlessness, for it was the name of a refuse dump outside Jerusalem where rubbish was burned. The Jewish prophets/ preachers took it as a metaphor to express the fate of the wicked, and Jesus took it over from them in this way. I certainly do not deny the danger of a judgment upon the wicked which may be pictured by such a metaphor. The point is – to what does the metaphor relate?

An important matter is the word *everlasting*, when linked with judgment. In this case, it is significant that the translators, since the AV, have replaced it with the word *eternal*.[11] This is significant because it is a translation of the adjective *aionios* (English *aeonian*), from *aion* (aeon, an age or epoch). The noun itself does not mean everlasting (see its use in Ephesians 3:11; 1:21). The adjective mens age-long, belonging to the ages, etc. It does not itself mean everlasting or endless, but sometimes, as when applied to God, it may be translated thus. This is because the meaning is inherent in the noun to which it is attached. In the Septuagint, which is the Greek version of the Old Testament which was used by the New Testament writers, this word *aionios* is often applied to things which are not everlasting, such as the priesthood of Aaron, David's kingdom, the Jerusalem temple, etc. So then, when the word is used of the punishment of future ages, it does not necessarily mean everlasting, and the use of the word *eternal* indicates here the *nature*, and not necessarily the *duration*, of the life or punishment in question.[12]

The matter which is beyond doubt is that the text itself (Matthew 25:46) simply says that the righteous shall go into *aeonion* life and the wicked into *aeonion* punishment – that is, life of the future age, and punishment of the future age, without specific reference to duration. The word is used in the Greek Septuagint, in Habakkuk 3:6, twice in the same verse, for the 'everlasting mountains' and the 'everlasting ways' of God.

Because we think of *eternal* as primarily meaning *endless*, duration before quality, we have therefore come to think of both the life of the redeemed and the punishment of the unredeemed as everlasting. But those who would press for everlasting punishment do not take the literal meaning of St Paul's words when he says: 'As in Adam *all* die, even so in Christ shall *all* be made alive.' Here they would make the first *all* inclusive of the whole human race, and limit the second *all* to the elect or the redeemed. Of course, if such punishment is thought to be death or annihilation, it would, in fact, be everlasting. But that does not mean everlasting, conscious punishment.

2. The theory of *Conditional Immortality* holds that all who do not attain to eternal life shall suffer loss, and fall into annihilation – what some have described as lapsing into non-being. This theory does not hold the natural immortality of the soul, questioning that the Bible teaches such a Platonic theory. Immortality comes to light through the Gospel, and therefore, the unredeemed simply do not attain to it. This theory does escape two difficulties. It is consistent with the judgment of evil and the final victory of the good, and it avoids the eternal dualism of an endless co-existence of good and evil.

A basic idea here is that if a person is so malignantly and incurably wicked, turning his back upon love, light and life, then he will 'lapse' into the opposites, which are hatred, darkness and death – a kind of dying or dwindling out of existence. This would be an everlasting punishment, a loss of God and heaven, and a 'destruction' from the presence of the Lord. This answers to the *Gehenna* metaphor, and the burning up of the chaff with unquenchable fire.

It must be admitted that many Christians of both Catholic and Evangelical persuasion have had recourse to the concept of annihilation, if not conditional immortality, because it delivers them from an intolerable doctrine of everlasting punishment. But it does seem to depend upon only part of the biblical evidence, and has to ignore or leave aside some important New Testament teaching.

3. The theory of *Universal Restoration* or *Universalism* holds that ultimately, all human souls will be saved. John Hick puts it thus:

God will eventually succeed in His purpose of winning all

> men to Himself in faith and love. That this is indeed God's purpose in relation to man is surely evident from the living revelation of that purpose in Jesus Christ. In his life we see at work in our human history 'God our Saviour, who desires all men to be saved and to come to the knowledge of the truth' (1 Timothy 2:3–4).

This theory avoids both the doctrine of everlasting torment, and the accusation that God's good purpose would have failed if the unredeemed were annihilated, or lapsed into non-being. If God's will is the salvation of all, and all are not finally saved, then Hick points out that his purpose and will would have failed, and God's creation would be permanently marred, failing to fulfil itself to perfection.

I have heard many people who hold one of the first two theories say that they would *like* to believe in the ultimate salvation of all, but that both scripture and reason forbid it. Scripture they see as indicating that many will take the broad road that leads to destruction, and reason they see as representing man's freedom – so that even God could not invade the freedom he has given without making man a mere puppet.

Hick asks the question whether God *can* eventually do for his creatures what he *wants* to do. Augustinian and Calvinist theology believes he *can* do it, but that he does not *desire* to do so, or perhaps it is better stated that whatever God willed for creation would infallibly be brought about by his sovereignty. But that means believing that God created some for salvation (the few), and the rest for damnation (most of the human race).

At this point I would recommend a careful reading of John Hick on 'Theodicy versus Hell', especially where he touches on this very point. It seems to him morally impossible that the infinite resourcefulness of infinite love, working in unlimited time, should be eternally frustrated, for he cannot envisage the creature rejecting the good for which it was made, when God presents it to him in an endless variety of ways.

To show that God is able to save without interfering with human freedom he recalls William James' analogy of two chess players, a novice and a world master. Even though the novice is free at every stage to make his own moves, it can be predicted with complete practical certainty that the master will eventually win. Whatever moves the novice makes in freedom, the master can respond to bring the game to the conclusion he desires, without any interference with the freedom of the novice. Hick points out that the drama of man's salvation is not a contest of wills or skills between God and man, for God has made man for himself, and he can find perfect fulfilment and happiness only in God. Therefore God is not trying to force or entice his creature against the grain of his nature, but to follow his deepest desire, which can only lead to God himself. God does not seek to subjugate but to liberate, so a better analogy is introduced, that of a psychotherapist leading a man to his proper maturity:

> The divine Therapist has perfect knowledge of each human heart, is infinitely wise in the healing of its ills, has unbounded love for the patient and unlimited time to devote to him. It remains theoretically possible that He will fail; but He will never cease to try, and we may (as it seems to me) have a full practical certainty that sooner or later he will succeed.[13]

There has always been a strain of universalism in the Church, from earliest times, and as the *Doctrine in the Church of England Report* of 1938 says, there must be room in the Church 'for those who hold that the love of God will at last win penitence and answering love from every soul that it has created'.

Such people do have scriptural support which is powerful[14], but there is another, and sterner, side to scripture[15], and all the evidence must be weighed in so vital and eternal a matter.

All shall be well

Is it then impossible to know, and must we observe a reverent agnosticism? My own path has taken me from (1), which was imposed upon me until I clearly and prayerfully searched and thought and felt for myself, to a vacillating but unsatisfactory movement between (2) and (3). I could not read the amazing eighth chapter of Romans without a strange upsurge of hope within my heart, and the impact of the saving Gospel, communicated through scripture and living experience, only substantiated that hope. When I discovered that there were others, of theological standing, who could affirm a larger hope, it caused me to rejoice, not simply because of freedom from crude and tyrannical conceptions of the God of sovereign love, but because I saw that I was not alone in my pilgrimage of prayerful understanding, and that:

> the love of God is broader than the measure of man's mind,
> and the heart of the Eternal is most infinitely kind.

I realise, as I write, that I see through a glass darkly at present, but that I shall know even as also I am known. Heaven and hell are contained within the mystery of God's love, and the time will come when *every* knee shall bow to Christ, in heaven, on earth and under the earth, and *every* tongue confess that Jesus Christ is Lord, to God the Father's glory.[16] And even as I look again at that explosive passage of St Paul in 1 Corinthians 15:25–28, I recall again Origen's interpretation of it:

> So then, when the end has been restored to the beginning, and the termination of things compared with their commencement, that condition of things will be re-established in which rational nature was placed, when it had no need to eat of the tree of knowledge of good and evil; so that when all feeling of wickedness has been removed, and the individual has been purified and

> cleansed, He who alone is the one good God becomes to him 'all', and that not in the case of a few individuals, or of a considerable number, but He Himself is 'all in all'. And when death shall no longer anywhere exist, nor the sting of death, nor any evil at all, then verily God will be 'all in all'.[17]

I recall too the universal implications of Charles Wesley's hymn on the sovereign grace and love of God:

> Thy sovereign grace to all extends,
>   Immense and unconfined,
> From age to age it never ends;
>   It reaches all mankind.
>
> Throughout the world its breadth is known,
>   Wide as infinity;
> So wide it never passed by one,
>   Or it had passed by me.[18]

Revelation of Divine Love

The universal vision of Origen has always been too much for the more cautious theologians of the Church, though there have always been those, especially of the Eastern tradition, who have been moved and stirred by such a cosmic revelation. It is almost too much to ask – that the whole cosmos will be redeemed, and that St Paul's vision of the groaning of creation in the eighth chapter of Romans be fulfilled in universal redemption. But light comes to us from a surprising source – the theological vision of a mediaeval woman, Lady Julian of Norwich.

The Revelations of Divine Love were vouchsafed to Lady Julian, the 14th century mystical writer, who communicated them with penetrating wisdom, grace and charm.[19] At one point, she had been much troubled by the Church's open teaching on the lost in hell, and found it impossible to believe that such a thing could be. Then as she puzzled and prayed, the Lord's word came to her: 'Everything is going to be all right.' And again: 'You will see for yourself that every sort of thing will be all right.' And in these two sayings she found rest, and came to see that the whole scheme of salvation would make *everything* right on a cosmic scale, and that the Lord cared about small things, and would show *her* that every *sort* of thing would fall into place, in spite of the impossibility of reconciling such teaching at the present moment.

The heart of this was a divine secret, a hidden counsel in the heart of God, which it was not possible for us to understand *now*, but which would be understood at the coming of Christ in glory, when this divine and cosmic secret would be revealed for our good and to his glory. Listen to her:

> So from those same six words 'I may make everything all right', I gain great comfort with regard to all the works that God has still to do. There still remains a deed which the blessed Trinity will do at the last Day – at least so I see it – yet when and how it will be done is unknown to all God's creatures under Christ, and will remain so until it takes place. The reason why he wants us to know about this deed is that he would have us more at ease in our minds and more at peace in our love, and not be concerned with those storms and stresses that stop us from truly enjoying him.

She still realises that this amazing deed of secret counsel will have to be as wonderful as the first creation, the potential of which is hidden within the heart of God, and treasured there. It is as if Julian is seeing into the heart of God, and there beholding a treasure and a secret that not only eases her mind but also rejoices her heart. She cannot tell or understand how the secret can possibly fulfil the promise, but she believes and trusts. She speaks again:

> This great deed, ordained by the Lord God from before time, and treasured and hid within his blessed heart, is known only to himself. By it he will make everything to turn out well. For just as the blessed Trinity made everything out of nothing, in the same way he shall make all that is wrong to turn out for the best.

And last of all, she says that no one can know it, no one is capable of knowing it, until the last day, for the secret is with Christ. But *when* it is done, then all that is now wrong will be made well. This is in accord not only with the great prophetic strain throughout the Bible, but with the restoration vision of the Eastern Fathers and the unitive wisdom of the mystical tradition of East and West.

It means that however dark the night of sin, and with no clue of hope or light upon the horizon, we have the secret wisdom and counsel of God. That amazing secret is at the heart of redemption, in the shape of a cross. For the top of the cross pierces the heart of God, the foot of the cross plumbs the very depths of hell, and the arms of the cross are open in invitation to the whole world.

The Man upon the cross is the nail-pierced Saviour, and God incarnate. His death is the death of death, and his cross is the gateway to eternal life, the destruction of all the powers of darkness and the continuing of never-ending joy.

> O Cross, that liftest up my head,
> I dare not ask to fly from thee;
> I lay in dust, life's glory dead,
> And from the ground there blossoms red
> Life that shall endless be.

Notes

1 John Macquarrie, *The Principles of Christian Theology* (London: SCM), pp. 366f.

2 John Hick, *Evil and the God of Love* (London: Collins Fontana), pp. 377f.
3 Revelation 20:11–15.
4 Matthew 25:31–46.
5 See John Baillie, *And the Life Everlasting* (London: OUP), pp. 237ff.; J. Paterson Smyth, *The Gospel of the Hereafter* (London: Hodder & Stoughton), pp. 202ff.
6 Acts 3:18–21 (NEB).
7 See Clement of Alexandria; Origen; Gregory of Nyssa. See Matthew 17:11; Acts 1:6; Ephesians 2:16; Colossians 1:20, 21, and its use in physical healing and restoration in Matthew 12:13; Mark 8:25.
8 *Soul Making* (London: SCM), pp. 9f.
9 J. Paterson Smyth, *op. cit*, pp. 204f.
10 *The Unutterable Beauty* (London: Hodder & Stoughton), p. 70.
11 See Matthew 25:46 in RSV, NEB, TEV, NIV, JB, etc.
12 F. D. Maurice, in *Eternal Life and Eternal Death* (1846), argued that 'eternal' in the NT did not mean 'of endless duration', drawing out the theological and practical implications. As a result he was dismissed from his chair at King's College, London. See 'Universalism' in Alan Richardson, *A New Dictionary of Christian Theology* (London: SCM), pp. 591f.
13 John Hick, *op. cit.*, pp. 377ff.
14 See, e.g. 1 Timothy 2:4; 2 Peter 3:9; Hebrews 6:7; John 12:31, 32; Luke 3:6; Titus 2:11; 1 Timothy 4:10; 1 John 2:2; 1 John 3:8 with Genesis 3:15; Luke 11:21, 22; Hebrews 9:26; Romans 12:25–33; Acts 3:21; 1 Corinthians 15:22–29.
15 Philippians 3:19; 2 Thessalonians 1:9; Matthew 26:24, etc.
16 Philippians 2:10, 11.
17 See Jaroslav Pelikan, *The Shape of Death* (London: Macmillan), p. 85f.
18 *Wesley's Hymns* (1779), No. 216.

19 Julian of Norwich, *Revelations of Divine Love*, trans. Clifton Wolters (Harmondsworth: Penguin Books), pp. 109–111.

Epilogue: Joy Comes in the Morning

The theme of joy has carried us, in this book, from creation and fall, through redemption, up to the borderlands of consummation, seeking to trace the joy of God in every department of our human lives. We have found joy in all forms of creativity and aesthetic and intellectual experience, and rejoiced in the vitality of communicative joy both in personal and corporate life. Such joy has been evident, not only in positive and liberating experiences, but also in the valleys of shadow, sickness and death. And in our approach to human mortality and finitude we have glimpsed the hope of eternal life, and the vision of union with God forever.

If eternal life is a present possession for the believer (and the New Testament assures us that it is), then we are already recipients of the graces of heaven. We know the joys of forgiveness and reconciliation, and the powers of the new birth into the Kingdom of God. By the indwelling of the Holy Spirit we have a foretaste and pledge of future glory, and in prayer and worship we enter, even now, into actual experience of the living God.

I have affirmed all the powers of the world to come in our present experience *in embryo*, but have also pointed to the reality and objectivity of the life hereafter. Death is the beginning of life in a new dimension, and the intermediate state of the soul in the loving and nearer presence of God, after death, is not the final state of resurrection in a new and immortal body, which is the future blessedness of the communion of saints at the coming of Christ in glory.

I have endeavoured to avoid a crude literalism in terms of time and space metaphors, while at the same time affirming the resurrection of Jesus in a transfigured, immortal and glorified body. If I were pressed to expound the meaning of those words I would be hard put to, because these are faith-affirmations in an entirely new and spiritual dimension. But I would still affirm their objective reality – the realisation of which will exceed all that we can hope for or imagine in our present physical, three-dimensional existence.

The empty tomb is not a matter for speculation but for celebration, and the fact that Jesus was no longer in the tomb means not only that he is 'existentially' present within the heart, but that he will bring to an end the present historical process at his coming in glory. He will initiate the Kingdom of God in *eschatological* (end-of-the-world) destruction and transfiguration, putting an end to evil and death. The temporal process, as we know it, will be no more, and all the prophetic promises of scripture, at present clothed in analogy, metaphor and parable, will be caught up in unimaginable wonder and ineffable glory.

Also, I have sought to affirm both the personal and corporate nature of our sharing in the divine glory. The stories of the Transfiguration and the Resurrection are the basis for our hope, reflected in one of the loveliest promises of the New Testament contained in the Epistle to the Philippians:

> Our commonwealth is in heaven, and from it we await a Saviour, the Lord Jesus Christ, who will change our lowly body, to be like his glorious body, by the power which enables him even to subject all things to himself.

So the theme of joy has been the golden thread throughout creation, redemption and consummation. The fulness of such joy is not yet. We have the foretaste, pledge, promise, hope, but the fulness yet awaits us. The anticipation of joy in God forever gives me joy in the present moment. My ecstasies and despairs in this mortal state are all bound up in such anticipation, and the restlessness of heart which I now experience is akin to the patient and impatient attitude of the lover who awaits the coming of the Beloved.

In this poor world we live in the darkness before dawn. We are assured that though our weeping may endure for a night, joy comes in the morning, and already the wide sky is heavy with anticipation and expectant longing, so that the last words of the Bible are entirely appropriate:

> He who testifies to these things says, 'Surely I am coming soon.' Amen. Come, Lord Jesus! The grace of the Lord Jesus be with all the saints. Amen.

Appendix: Music, Meditation and Action

It is extremely difficult to select music for particular meditation-themes, and in any case, you will have your own music preferences and resources, and there are whole catalogues of meditation music now available.* The following selection will give you some possible ideas, but care must be taken to make space and silence, and not let the music intrude or take over. There is also literature available but a simple pattern I learned from the Cowley Fathers runs:

1. Stillness of Body
2. Inspiration by the Spirit
3. Concentration with Christ
4. Silence in God.

The music may precede, accompany or follow the meditation, but there should be adequate time of silence. The action commended is again only suggestive. The Lord will indicate particular actions to you as a result of your meditation. Don't be legalistic or stilted, but allow the discipline of meditation to flow into spontaneity.

Chapter 1. Creation: The Dance of Joy
Music: Bach: Double Concerto in D Minor.
Meditation: Make the two quotations by Abhishiktananda in the chapter the substance of your meditation, and repeat

*A whole series of over 150 music cassettes for meditation (plus a Gregorian Chant series) are available from New World Cassettes, Strawberry Vale, Twickenham TW1 1BR – catalogue free.

slowly, audibly but quietly those thoughts to which your spirit responds. Then rest within the divine presence, and breathe the beauty of the pattern and harmony of the Holy Spirit in the unfolding of creation.
Action: Do a walking, awareness meditation. Respond to the divine life in the country, seaside or parkland chosen. Let your physical walking, moving, breathing, watching, listening, smelling, touching – all be taken up into the meditation. And let this be the beginning of a new awareness of the life and joy of God in the created order.

Chapter 2. Alienation: The Loss of Joy
Music: Allegri: Miserere.
Meditation: Consider William Blake's poem 'The Poison Tree', reviewing your own relationships over the years. Have you discovered and faced the anger hidden within yourself – towards God, towards others? Is the Gospel working its reconciling power in your life? Let the Lord show you those painful, unhealed wounds and memories which you have evaded for so long. But don't wallow in self-pity or guilt. Rather, allow yourself to be exposed to the healing of his loving presence.
Action: Don't attempt too much, thereby becoming discouraged, but take a simple step of reconciliation in a marred personal relationship today – perhaps a word or a letter. Or bring joy to a lonely or depressed person in your neighbourhood.

Chapter 3. Redemption: The Recovery of Joy
Music: Bach: Brandenburg Concerto No. 1.
Meditation: Reflect upon, or sing, the hymns of the chapter:

> Fairest Lord Jesus
> Just as I am, without one plea
> Just as I am, Thine own to be

and allow the devotional-theological themes of the hymns to saturate your being.

Action: Find out some information about a suffering person or group through Amnesty International or similar organisation, and write or contribute towards the alleviation of their suffering.

Chapter 4. Triune Love: The Source of Joy
Music: Bruch: Violin Concerto.
Meditation: Base your meditation on Acts 10:38, quoted in the chapter. Reflect upon the power of God given to Jesus by the Spirit's anointing, and its manifestation in all his acts of compassion and healing. Then open yourself to the indwelling and anointing of the same Spirit – and offer thanks and praise to the Father.
Action: Write out, repeat and learn the text. Live today in the immense potential of its activity in your own life, and let the beauty of Jesus be manifested in you.

Chapter 5. Joy: Inheritance of Our Humanity
Music: Bach: Air from Suite No. 3 in D.
Meditation: Compare the pre-Christian meditation 'The Breath of Nature' with St Patrick's Breastplate (full version *English Hymnal* 212), both in the chapter, and discover the same Holy Spirit present and working at all times and in all places, as the Lord and giver of life.
Action: Seek to understand the universality of God's gracious love in the world, and learn to practise a new open graciousness to those of other faiths, see not only to share the riches of Jesus, but to discover the Holy Spirit's presence in them, thus widening the horizons of joy.

Chapter 6. Joy: Maturing through Suffering
Music: Albinoni: Adagio for Organ and Strings.
Meditation: In the light of this chapter reflect on the words: 'Perhaps forgiveness is one of the greatest signs of maturity, for it includes understanding and discernment, and is free from revenge and hatred.' Then consider your life and

attitude by these words, and ask for grace to practise the implications of your meditation.

Action: Has your suffering led to rebellion, hatred and self-pity! Is it possible to allow it to lead you into a greater maturity! God does not send suffering, but in permitting it gives opportunity for healing, maturity and perhaps deliverance. Resolve to be more compassionate and discerning both with your own and others' suffering and endeavour to show maturity in your evaluation and judgment of others.

Chapter 7. Joy: Personal and Corporate

Music: Mozart: Flute Concerto No. 2.

Meditation: Spend some time in the slow perusal of the poem 'What the Soul Desires', in the chapter. Then meditate upon the quotations from Dietrich Bonhoeffer.

Action: Ask yourself these two questions:

Do I know the meaning of solitude in terms of duration and depth?

Do I engage in loving community sharing in the Church and the world?

And act in answer to these questions. It may mean integrating regular solitude into your life, and giving time, talents or money to social concerns such as Amnesty International, Red Cross, Oxfam, or supporting medical, educational or missionary work on a regular and responsible basis.

Chapter 8. Joy: A Contemplative Perspective

Music: Pachelbel: Canon

Meditation: Travel in imagination with the novice mentioned in the chapter, above the frenetic activity of your own life, up into the height of the mountain of stillness and prayer. Observe the beauty of the surroundings as you climb, and the twisting of the simple, ascending path. Then view the panoramic and widening horizon all around, until you reach the summit. Lie down and gaze into the sky, and remain there for up to fifteen minutes. Then consider the 'contemplative

perspective' envisaged by Thomas Merton in the quotations of the chapter, and ask if this is the perspective of your own life.
Action: For the next few days begin the day reviewing the above meditation, and each day integrate such a perspective into your day's events. Affirm positively the compassion of such a perspective as events occur. Do not *impose* but *respond.* Do not *initiate* but *reciprocate*–and in such flowing co-operation be aware of the resulting joy!

Chapter 9. Awareness of Spiritual Vitality
Music: Vaughan Williams: Five Mystical Songs.
Meditation: Recall an area in which vitality has brought you joy in life–physically, mentally or spiritually. Recapture the experience in quiet meditation by imagining reliving the physical thing (from swimming, to pottery or teamwork); reflecting upon the intellectual/aesthetic thing (from creative composition to the solving of an intricate problem); or recalling the spiritual experience in the loving awareness of God's presence. Now read again that section of the chapter entitled 'The Pearl of Greatest Price', or, better still, get someone to read it within a group.
Action: Be open again to those vital and creative periods of your life, allowing God to renew them within you. Affirm that you can be converted, inspired and filled anew with the Spirit's creative energies, working in appropriate ways for your present life. Then return to practical ways of integrating such powers, taking counsel from a soul-friend or spiritual guide, sharing the substance of this chapter and your reflections.

Chapter 10. Communicating Joy
Music: Beethoven: Symphony No 9 (Schiller's 'Ode to Joy').
Meditation: Read slowly two extracts from the chapter:
The poem 'Christ in You'
The joy and communication shared with Bob.
Have you ever experienced communicative joy with

another/others? Do you reckon such experience to be part of the Christian life! Are you simple, open, loving enough for it to be part of your experience? Are you willing for it? Consider the cost. Now are you willing?
Action: From today, be open to all that is good and creative in the world, and be prepared to receive joy. If and when you experience joy, let it flow. Don't possess, covet, grasp or hang on to it, but let it come, let it go, spread it around. Voice and act out your gratitude to God – sing, shout, dance and live in Gospel joy.

Chapter 11. Joy in Life and Death
Music: Bach: Et Resurrexit from the B Minor Mass.
Meditation: Lie down upon the floor. Cross your hands over your chest and relax with quiet, slow, deep breathing, and reflect upon your own mortality and death. Think about your loneliness in life and death; then think about the communion of saints in life and death. Read the Wesley hymn 'Rejoice for a brother deceased', from the chapter, and ask if it finds an echo in your longing and experience.
Action: Take a meditative walk into the countryside. Note the season of the year and reflect upon the appropriate seasonal signs (springtime, new life; summer, full bloom; autumn, fruitfulness and maturity; winter, darkness and death). Learn the lessons of your finitude and mortality and affirm by faith the life which survives physical death in Christ. Learn too that since death is imminent and universal, there is no place for hatred and violence, for revenge and avarice, for ambition or manipulative power. As you walk, walk in the Spirit of reconciliation and eternal life.

Chapter 12. Joy in Crossing Over
Music: Elgar; 'Go Forth upon thy Journey', from *The Dream of Gerontius*.
Meditation: Integrate your meditation with the poetry and music of *The Dream of Gerontius*, reflecting upon the teaching of the extracts in the chapter.

Action: Be more aware of loving nursing and pastoral work for the dying. Find out more about and support in an appropriate manner the work of your local hospital chaplain and hospice for the terminally ill. Let the fact of your death be woven into the manner of your life, and let the joy of God suffuse both. Realise that your death may be nearer than you think; pray about it and give thanks for it. Pray for all who will be affected by it – and all within the undergirding of the love of God.

Chapter 13. Judgment and Eternal Joy
Music: Fauré: Requiem.
Meditation: Read slowly again the last section of the chapter, giving attention to the extracts from Lady Julian. Pray for all souls, reflecting upon the judgment and the compassion of God which manifest the two sides of the divine Love. Surrender all fear and doubt to the Lord, affirming as his child that 'all will be well' because ultimately the divine Love will be victorious, and God the Father will be 'all in all'.
Action: Make a list of all those you have loved in your life who have died. Hold them lovingly in the presence of God, remembering them especially at the next celebration of the holy eucharist. Make next All Saints' Day and All Souls' Day (1st and 2nd November) particular days of remembrance and celebration for the departed. And finally, reflect that the best of earthly joys reflect something of the glory of the life to come, where the Lamb will be the light, in the glory of the Father.